About the author

Rich Hardy has been a professional environment and animal protection activist for twenty-five years. He has led campaigns for some of Britain's most creative and successful non-profit organisations including Surfers Against Sewage, cleaning up Europe's coastlines and starting their fight against ocean plastic; and Veganuary, a pledge campaign that inspired a quarter of a million people worldwide to try a vegan diet in 2019.

But all the while, over the course of two decades, he's been going undercover to document the animals that suffer for human gain. His images and testimony have fuelled the work of more than twenty international animal protection organisations. These high-risk endeavours saw him awarded a prestigious *Daily Mirror* 'Special Recognition Animal Hero Award' in 2019.

Praise for *Not As Nature Intended*

'Cruelty to animals goes on daily behind the closed doors of factory farms or deep in the forests where wild animals are trapped for their fur. Rich's book exposes us to the raw truth behind these animal trades. Whilst it's a deeply personal story, it has the potential to change, not just your own life, but the lives of millions of animals. I urge you to read it!'
Joanna Lumley, Actress, author and activist

'It is beautifully and lucidly written… it avoids gratuitous expression but delivers the truth in a compelling and penetrating narrative. "Not As Nature Intended" is a must read.'
Peter Egan, Actor and animal advocate

'A 007 of the animal world.'
Rhian Lubin, *The Daily Mirror*

'As you read this book, if you have a heart and a soul, you too won't fail to be bowled over by Rich's courage.'
Jane Dalton, *The Independent*

'All the evidence we need to make our future a plant-based one.'
Christina Rees MP , Chair of the All-Party Parliamentary Group on Vegetarianism and Veganism

'An eye-opening insight into the horrors endured by animals around the world – and into the minds of those who risk everything to help them.'
Maria Chiorando, *Plant Based News*

Not As Nature Intended

Not As Nature Intended

Rich Hardy

unbound

This edition first published in 2020

Unbound
6th Floor Mutual House, 70 Conduit Street, London W1S 2GF
www.unbound.com
All rights reserved

Chapter illustrations by Vita Sleigh

vitasleigh.com

@vitasleigh

ISBN (eBook): 978-1-78965-064-8
ISBN (Paperback): 978-1-78965-063-1

Cover design by Mecob

Printed and bound in Great Britain by Clays Ltd, Elcograf S.p.A.

For the raccoon who died in a freezing river at the hands of a cruel man. I still think of that brave animal every day.

And to my beloved Pru, for having the strength to go undercover for animals with me – and confront the industries responsible for animal suffering – and for her love, support and constant encouragement in helping me write this book and make sure I tell this story.

Super Patrons

Susanne Abetti
Mandi Adams
Stacy Adkins
Mark Adrien Richards
Animal Aid
Anthony Aitman
Elizabeth Allen
Ann Allen
Reece Almquist
White & Schrader
Benny Andersson
Moe Asari
Martin Ashby
Alex Atwater
Sophie Baden
Tor Bailey
David Baillie
Sofia Balderson
Lewis Banks
Jonathan Baty
Martin Bay
Janice Beckinsale
Nikki Bednall
Jocelyn Beggs
Jon Bennett
Sovay Berriman
Elisa Bianco
Becky Bolton
Danny Bond
Victoria Bond

Bryan Borek
Natasha Boyland
Vendula Brabcová
Lydia Bradford
Sally Branch
Rhiannon Bresnitz
Antoinette Broadhead
Rachida Brocklehurst
Rachel Brookman
Noreen Brosnanc
Becca Brown
Casey Brown
Alex Bugden
Kristle Butcher
Jeremey Cacciola
James Camp
Rebecca Cappelli
Sharida M Caras
Anthony Carpendale
Julia Ceri Jones
Daniel Chalmers
Georgina Charlesworth
Diana Cimino
Gregory Cohen
Jordan Collins
Victoria Conner
Cassie Connolly
Annabel Cowper
Mark Cox
Mary R. Crumpton

Andy Cummins
Cort Cunningham
Isobel Davies
Carolyn Dayton
Rosemary Dean
Lachlan Denneny
Danfung Dennis
Gabriella Di Caprio
Niki di Palma
Michelle Douglas
Roxanne Dufour Cantin
Anastasiya Dusova
David Ebert
Jowan Edwards
Marlene Eisenhauer
Aida Elise
Pru Elliott
Tim Elliott
Dave Ellis
Skye Elmore
Charlotta Eriksson
Fatema Faith
Aaron Faith
McKenzie Farrell
Krysia Fenwick-Loye
Katie Ferneyhough
Samantha Ferry
Casey Fisher
Cara FitzMaurice
Filming For Liberation
Christine Fuglestad
Mariany Gainza Perez
Marian Gale-Batten
Leah Garcés
Vic Garner
Lana Garrison
Talulah Gaunt
Romina Giel
Nicola Glen
Matthew Glover
Lynn Gober
Bob Gobey
Emma Goddard
Lúcia Gomes Pereira
Suzanne Goodwin
Simon Griffiths

Nicola Guernari
Kerry Hardy
Mara Hardy
Gordon Hardy
Sue Hartley
Katie Havlitschek
Dara Hayes
Olivia Hazell
Katie Hickman
Lianne Hicks
Amanda Hignett
Trina Ho
Katie Hopkins
richard houck
Rob Howells
Gemma Huckerby
Rachel Huff-Wagenborg
andy hughes
Staci Hurley
Animals Innocent
Anne James-Burns
Kim Jepheart
Jessicah Jones
Airi Kanazawa
Laura Keeran
Christina Kennedy
Dan Kieran
Olga Kikou
Olivia King
Michael Kirby
Rachel Kisley
Rebecca Knowles
Ereania Kowalczyk
Marlena   Kropidłowska-Okraska
Jakob Kummetz
Alex Leah Johnston
Minyoung Lee
@letusbeheroes
Tracey Lindop
Amanda Lyons
Tess Macpherson-Woods
Daniel MacRae
Mythili Mahendran
Sophie Mariner
Donna Marino

Jax Martone

Rosalind Mason – nee Hinton

George Mathios

Sophie Mathy

Tom McCaffrey

Julie McCartan

Julie Meredith

Silvia Meriggi

Tabitha Metcalfe

John Mitchinson

Rosa Moegel de Basauri

Helen Molendijk

Tom & Mandy Moseley

Kelly Myers

Sara Nash

Kelly Neale

Claudia Neto

Sarah Nicole Robertson

Monica C Nilsen

Natalie No

Caroline Nobee

Blue Norman

Christina O'Neill

Eileen Obrien

Katrin Øien

Mika Otsuka

Alice Oven

Tessa Padilla

Mila Palma

Karen Peper

Kelley Perry

Lou Pete

Hana Platková

Justin Pollard

Charlie Pritchard

Andrew Qaqiesh

Essie Quinlivan

Vicki Reid

Marietheres Reinke

Michelle Remin

Lara Richardson

Kim Richardson

Kaicee Robertson

Selena Rosario

Lisette Rotman

Martha Rowen

Fiona Russek

Niccolina Ryon

Mariana Salerno

Greta Sarasi

Billie Savage

Menno Schaaf

Julie Sheppard

Leslie Shuber

Carina Skov Korsgaard

Phil Sleigh

Citlali Sofie Gerits

Lili Soh

Catherine Sorley

Filip Stachnik

Jake Staples

Rebecca Stewart

Saskia Storey

Alex Suchy

Vanda Sudic

Marcin Tabaszewski

Hugo Tagholm

Johann Taylor

Tora Teig

Rosalind Tendler

Chelsea Thorne

Pia K Töre-Wallin

Anna Travinskaya

Grace Twiston-Davies

Cheryl Valdez

Gaby van Bienen

Pascalle van Stralen

vp4a.com

Zining Wang

Tina Warren

Philip Waters

Hannah Watkins

Wendy Watts

Zach Weigel

Moritz Weresow

Jeffrey Whaley

Kelsy White

Nancy Williams

Simon Winch

Amy Winkler

Doris Witter

Karmen Wong
Hannah Yates
Osman Yavas

Jon Young
Katie Zarajczyk
Roberta Zuanon

With special thanks to Veganuary

Veganuary inspires and supports people to go vegan – one of the most effective choices a person can make to reduce the suffering of animals, help the planet and improve personal health. Veganuary is dedicated to changing public attitudes and behaviours, while providing all the information and practical support required to make the transition to veganism as easy and enjoyable as possible.

veganuary.com

Contents

Foreword

I read quite a lot of books. And in recent years I've been kindly asked to write a fair few forewords. Obviously I always read the book before I start writing, as I did this book. The problem was that when I finished it I had no idea how and where to begin. And when you read it you will understand why.

Rich's book is well written, well crafted. . . his style is engaging and his stories are gripping. But while this is all essential in any book, in this case it is completely and utterly overwhelmed by the content. The content is extremely powerful, in fact it is devastating in its impact. I had to read much of it two or three times just to get it clearly into my mind. And then I spent the rest of the day or night thinking and rethinking about it. I wanted it to be unbelievable, so I had to spend time making myself believe it. Not that there is any doubt in its veracity, just that its unflinching, brutal truths are things that we all don't want to know. And that wilful blindness, that sheepish comfort in ignorance is paid for with horrific cost – not by us readers, humans, but by the abject suffering of the millions of other animals whose miserable lives and deaths are detailed here.

It will be easy for these accounts to make the reader dislike the people whose callous disregard for life and unspeakable cruelty are the cause of such suffering. Their crimes are of such a magnitude that it will for some no doubt prompt a ferocious loathing for our entire species. Maybe that's a forgivable reaction, but I had another, because at the centre of all this inhumanity is a truly remarkable human – Rich Hardy.

His dedication, his stoicism, his determination, his relentless energy to expose the horrors wrought upon the pitiful victims of abuse around the world, and most admirable of all, his mental capacity to somehow absorb and manage his experiences, are quite beyond comprehension. Not to mention his selfless bravery. I don't do hugs, but when I closed this book I wanted to put my coat on and go find Rich wherever he was in the world and shake his hand very, very vigorously and say thank you. I felt an enormous personal debt to him and a level of appreciation that was dizzying. He is a true hero, an outstanding man, someone who has immeasurably improved the lives of animals everywhere on earth.

So yes, reading this is going to hurt. I've read things in these pages which I will never forget, so I can't lie and say you won't be moved, angered or scarred by these accounts. But it is absolutely imperative that you read this book. Not simply in order to honour Rich's endeavours, but because without an awareness of these despicable practices you will never be sufficiently moved to take the actions required to stop them. And to that end this book is not only important, it is essentially empowering. This is a book which can and must change the world for millions of animals, and now both it and that mission are in your hands. So please read it and make that happen.

Chris Packham, New Forest, 2019

Prologue

I watched the silhouettes of five dolphins rear up in the wave face and then go left as I stroked over the top of the breaking wave.

Just as I had harnessed the previous wave's energy to race down the line, using the fins of my surfboard to spray droplets of water back into their salty home, these creatures were here for the same reason, to surf the waves – pure enjoyment.

And it wasn't just the dolphins. Nature was throwing a party. Seabirds were base-jumping from nearby cliffs, their long beaks splitting the water's surface with minimal disruption. Fish leaped and fronds of kelp waved at me as I duck-dived my board under and through the lip of every watery chandelier that broke in front of me. Surfing was my release. It still is. It provides me with an opportunity to see the best of what nature has to offer, even at a time when nature is taking a battering at the hands of humans. But that day, despite all that awe and wonder, I couldn't shake off the sight of the giant sheds on the road running down to the beach, or the tell-tale, foul-smelling odour above them. I hadn't expected to find a factory farm in such an idyllic spot.

As a professional campaigner working on behalf of animal organisations for nearly a decade, I was very aware of what was inside those sheds – hens, tens of thousands of them. Each one genetically selected to put every ounce of energy they could muster into the production of an egg a day – an egg so clean, and so perfect, surely it could only be laid by prize hens, living the most lavish of chicken lives? Not so. I knew that these hens were kept locked up in battery cages so small, they couldn't even stretch their wings.

I had taken a year off from campaigning to go to New Zealand, exploring remote sections of the East Coast and seeking out lonely waves to surf. Just a few months earlier, my colleagues and I had secured a monumental campaign victory that saw the European Union outlaw the use of barren battery cages for egg-laying hens. Ultimately, those barren cages were replaced with a so-called 'enriched' cage, which offered some basic improvements in the form of a nest box, perches and a dust-bathing area.[1] Of course, enriched cages were never going to be the answer – a cage is still a cage – but getting any factory farming system banned was a huge challenge. To end one of the worst examples of factory farming, and to see the industry have to shell out huge sums of money to change their systems (it cost £400 million in the UK alone)[2], was worth celebrating. It offered hope and showed the industry that change was coming – and they were going to have to pay for it.

It was a victory hard won, and I was exhausted. Working full time on that campaign had taken everything out of me,

1. https://www.bhwt.org.uk/egg-industry/enriched-cages/
2. https://www.foodsafetynews.com/2012/01/european-union-bans-battery-cages-for-egg-laying-hens/

and I needed a recharge before I could contemplate returning to more work for animals. So I dusted down my surfboard and travelled to New Zealand, the first stop in what would be a year-long surf trip. A few days later, and having parted with a good chunk of dollars to buy a beaten-up Mitsubishi van in which to live and travel, I was sitting on my board beyond the breaking waves. A lull in the waves had got me reflecting on the hens in those sheds. During the campaigning period, I had undertaken a lot of talks and given interviews in the media about why it was wrong to keep hens in battery cages. I had a convincing patter and knew all the scientific and ethical arguments, but I had never actually seen hens in cages for myself. I considered this a weakness when it came to lobbying and, on several occasions, this was underlined when I was undermined by the opposition and also by decision-makers capable of creating change for hens. And, while the campaign had been successful, there weren't vast banks of film footage available to reference, so campaigners were very reliant on written evidence – such as scientific reports – to make their case. I couldn't help thinking that, if there were more imagery available to show people and politicians what life was really like inside these dreadful factory farms, it might be possible to speed up the rate of change.

The next set of waves came through and I paddled hard for the first wave. The lip threw out far enough for me to sneak inside the barrel, and, for a split second, I was enveloped in the swirling, watery mass. On exiting, instead of continuing down the green wall that was offering a much longer ride, I directed my board towards the beach. Even though I was on holiday, I was going to that farm above the beach, and I was going to look inside. I felt this was something I could – and had to – do for myself.

With hair still dripping wet, I parked the van in a lay-by.

Without looking for a towel, I peeled off my wetsuit and grabbed my video camera from the footwell of the passenger seat before I could change my mind. I didn't really look after it very well. It was always getting a battering from extreme weather while documenting the surf trips I was making. As I walked towards the farm, I frantically rubbed grains of sand and surf wax from its outer casing and cleaned the lens with my t-shirt. All seemed quiet. It was lunchtime, so perhaps the workers were eating in the main house.

I knew that hundreds of thousands of dollars were spent on building factory farms like this, to keep the hens in and the public out. Designed like a fortress, this one had no windows and really offered no clues as to what was on the inside if you were an outsider. Long, dark shadows cast from the tall buildings, which incarcerated the unfortunate hens, smothered the ground. It was a foreboding place. Set back from a rural road and with no close neighbours, its considered positioning would normally be enough to keep the animals out of sight and out of mind, but not today.

Despite all the investment, the physical barriers and the foreboding atmosphere, it was the lack of a simple NZ$10 padlock that enabled me to get inside. Without even considering what I would say if I were confronted, I slid back the giant door of one of the sheds. I instinctively flipped the toggle of the camera to record and its little red light lit up a pathway in the darkness for me to follow.

While the light level was low, the noise was not. Though I couldn't yet see them, I could hear squawking and the flapping of wings against metal from beyond another steel door. It was unlocked. I looked back over my shoulder. Still no one, so I opened the door.

Like high-rise flats, the battery cages rose up all around me in every direction. I suddenly felt quite small amongst them and found my eyes straining in the poor light to judge how far back they went. It was a long way – too long to calculate from inside.

Feathers were falling from the highest tiers and hens were taking it in turns to jut out their scrawny necks through gaps in the cage bars. Just as I would frequently strain to come up for air after being pile-driven beneath the surface of the sea from a particularly fearsome wave, it struck me that these birds were doing something similar. It felt like it was freedom they were reaching out for. With wide eyes and gaping beaks, they grabbed brief moments away from the cage before a cage mate jostled them out of position for their turn. On and on it went down the aisle. Like a cash register springing into action, thousands of hens were trying to escape from the wire mesh prisons they were forced to endure for their eighteen-month life – such a short and miserable life for a bird that could in a natural setting live for eight to ten years.[3]

This barren system forms the foundation for how factory farming works. It is completely reliant on cages, crates or vast indoor warehouses where animals are packed in at the highest stocking densities. They restrict space and, by doing so, deny natural animal behaviour. It is this system that produces the bulk of the world's meat, eggs and dairy.

Their overgrown claws curled around the sloping wire floors of their cages. Their bodies were a fifty-fifty mix of feathers and sore skin. I already knew this was not a natural moult, though. Feathers were pulled out by each other, through a combination of stress and boredom. To mitigate the damage this caused, the farmer had made sure all his hens had arrived with beaks trimmed. A painful, but legal, process car-

3. https://www.mypetchicken.com/backyard-chickens/chicken-help/How-long-do-chickens-live-H106.aspx

ried out with a red-hot blade, this was an industry solution to preventing the worst injuries from hens pecking at each other.

Halfway down the aisle, I found my first corpse. Rotting in a far corner of the cage, it must have been here for days. I couldn't imagine trying to check these cages each day for birds that had fallen sick or were injured. It would be a huge job. I looked at my watch. Twenty minutes had passed since I had entered the shed and started filming. How long would workers stop for lunch? An hour, thirty minutes perhaps. I decided it was probably time to leave. I turned and made my way back towards the big door. I found myself saying, 'sorry', not once, but a few times as I passed by each cage. I knew it wasn't enough but it was the only thing I could do at that moment. I was upset and could feel my emotions were close to the surface. Talking to the hens somehow helped me stay composed.

The door slid back easily, but it was not my hand pulling the giant handle. Instead, I was hastily bundling the camera into my jacket pocket. I came face-to-face with a tall red-haired man, who could just as easily have played for the All Blacks instead of rearing hens.

'G'day,' I said.

'What are you doing in here?' he asked.

'I was looking for you… I, er, wanted to buy some eggs.'

The farmer looked me up and down a few times suspiciously.

'Well, you won't find them for sale in here.' He ushered me outside and shut the door.

What ensued was a little back and forth about trespassing on his property.

'My eggs can't be bought on site,' he said. 'A truck collects them and then they get distributed all across the country.'

'Right,' I said.

'And I don't like people I don't know coming onto my farm,' he added.

'Sorry,' I said, as a way of not escalating the situation.

I'd had a reprimand, but it was nothing more than a slap on the wrist. 'Red' escorted me to the main gate and then, with arms crossed, remained vigilant as I returned to my van and drove away.

I felt the warmth of the camera in my pocket and knew I had just recorded something with campaigning value. I had also surprised myself by thinking quickly on my feet and by managing to capture something I'd not seen before when campaigning for Europe's hens. I had followed my instinct and the belief that to make a difference for animals you had to tell their story. For me, that started with taking their picture and recording their life.

Taking a few minutes to process what I'd just seen, it was much clearer to me now why those official requests I'd made in the past to visit hen farms in the UK had been rebuffed. These really were not places the public would enjoy visiting and the egg industry already knew that.

Sitting in the driver seat of my van, hands still clasped firmly around my camera, I realised I could and should do more than just say 'sorry' to these hens. After all, I had evidence of their suffering. I pulled out the crumpled map of New Zealand that was stashed in the dashboard and added an 'X' to mark the spot on 'Auckland'. I would have to travel to the big city to find the nation's animal rights community – people just like me, people who wanted to make a difference to the lives of animals, to show others their suffering and lobby for change. Like me, such people felt that animals deserved much more than a factory farm; they recognised that animals are 'sentient', experience a range of emotions and feelings and can form relationships with fellow animals and humans, too. And, as it turned out, they valued the imagery I'd captured and vowed to make sure it was seen.

The next day I was back in the line-up. A new surf spot and some memorable waves welcomed me back into the sea, a place I'd always felt at home. No dolphins that day, but that was understandable. I think they know they can't trust humans; nor should they, given what we've done to so many of our fellow creatures.

Bobbing up and down on my board, alone except for my thoughts, I began planning for a new way of working to help animals – exploring a little-used method at that time for evidence-gathering. I was going to go undercover. I would combine secret filming with storytelling to campaign for change; I'd become someone who'd go to dark places to bring issues to light. I would document rather than openly advocate. I knew it would be a lonely experience but out here now, in the raw ocean, I was always comfortable and happy in my own company.

*

A year later I was back home in the UK. I'd saved a few pennies working on New Zealand fruit farms and I invested it in some cameras, making sure they were small enough to stash in my pocket if needed. My experience in that battery farm in New Zealand sent me on a twenty-year undercover journey to document and expose the suffering that animals endure to provide us with our food, fashion and entertainment.

My first assignment was for an NPO (non-profit organisation) campaigning to stop live animal exports across Europe. I joined a small team of investigators trailing livestock trucks as they travelled to farms and slaughterhouses in southern Spain. Soaring summer temperatures, faulty water systems and trucks failing to rest animals properly were documented; and European law – to protect the welfare of live animals during transport – was not just broken but shown as lacking and unenforceable. It was an emotional experience, but one I would have to get used to.

I knew when I started this journey that there was a long road ahead, full of injustices to document and expose, and that my efforts would be just one part of the solution. A lot has changed since I started this work, but there is still a lot left to change if we are to help animals, our planet and ourselves.

The Intergovernmental Panel on Climate Change reported that a huge reduction in meat and dairy consumption is essential to avoid climate breakdown,[4] yet globally each year we farm 70 billion animals for meat, milk or eggs, with two out of every three farm animals now factory-farmed.[5] And that's just on land. As many as 120 billion fish are thought to be intensively farmed in the world's seas and oceans.[6] Wild animals, in their millions, continue to be caught and killed in traps for their fur each year and more than 100 million remain incarcerated in fur farms.[7] And of the 195 countries in the world, only 26 have bans on wild animal circuses.[8]

The following stories you will read are based on the extracts of my investigation journals. They are just a few of many, but I feel they best represent the type of issues I've documented and the challenges and adversities typically experienced when spending long periods of time working undercover.

4. https://www.theguardian.com/environment/2018/oct/10/huge-reduction-in-meat-eating-essential-to-avoid-climate-breakdown

5. https://www.ciwf.org.uk/media/3640540/ciwf_strategic_plan_20132017.pdf

6. https://www.ciwf.org.uk/farm-animals/fish/

7. https://www.furfreealliance.com/fur-farming/

8. https://www.peta.org.uk/blog/these-26-countries-that-have-banned-wild-animal-circuses-are-making-england-look-really-bad/

I have been careful to omit exact locations and to change people's names in order to avoid personal retaliation from the people and industries that have been the subjects of these investigations. Aside from that, these encounters are a true representation of what life is like as an undercover investigator working on behalf of animals.

Yours with the animals,
Rich

Hidden in Plain Sight

'You want me to train lions?'

'Well, not exactly, but that could be your cover story,' said the voice at the other end of the phone.

My colleague looked up from her desk, and watched me suspiciously until I finished the call with my client, an international animal charity.

'Another project for Ace Ventura?' she jested.

'Something like that.'

***

We were working late. It was my last week running Surfers Against Sewage (SAS), the British clean seas campaigning group that I had loved leading for the past five years. It wasn't the first time my colleagues had overheard unusual, secretive conversations. I'd been going undercover during my 'holidays' the whole time I'd been with SAS and my colleagues understood the drill – even if they asked questions, I couldn't tell them what was planned. Whenever I took time off – even if they knew it was a *real* holiday – I'd come back to a barrage of merciless 007 jokes.

I packed away my wetsuit and set about joining a circus in mainland Europe – a continent where there were still countries that allowed wild animals to perform legally in circuses. Getting backstage and into the guarded working lives of those involved in running an animal circus would be no easy feat. My assignment was to find a way in, so I could secretly document how these animals were forced to live and work, both in and outside the circus ring.

I'd always enjoyed clowning around with friends, but the thought of spending time with people who train exotic – and often dangerous – animals to make them perform in front of hundreds of people made me more than a little uncomfortable.

2

I found animal circuses deeply distasteful but I resolved to do what was necessary to get close to those who made a career out of breaking the spirits of animals through their lifetime confinement.

Over the following days, I thought a lot about the approach I would take for this assignment. How could I get backstage from ringside and what would it look like there? I flexed my double-jointed thumbs and flicked them backwards and forwards but they were clearly not impressive enough to get me in as a contortionist. I had a decent beard but I hadn't seen any vacancies for a bearded man on the circus career websites. Aside from enrolling in a circus school, the best advice I'd found on joining a travelling circus was to apply or enquire in person. With that in mind, I hopped on a boat and crossed the English Channel to begin knocking on doors.

Europe was home to a multitude of travelling circuses. The largest toured all over, travelling in vast convoys of brightly coloured vehicles. They hauled their exotic cargoes in so-called 'beast wagons' tethered to the back of powerful trucks. The trucks were heavily branded, usually with the circus name bursting out in a 3D explosion alongside giant decals of tigers and trapeze artists. Everyone knew when the circus was in town.

Before I'd left, I'd spoken with some campaigners who were working hard to ban animal circuses across Europe, and I'd been given a few names of some of the people who train and supply dangerous wild animals to circuses and the entertainment industry. I decided it was wise to start this assignment by contacting some of those individuals before I turned up with my suitcase outside the big top, wanting to train as a lion tamer.

A few days later I found myself driving through a sleepy village. It had a bakery, a pharmacy and a small church. Rural villages are quiet at the best of times but, today, without a breath of wind, this place seemed especially still.

Victor's house was nothing special. A small mid-terrace building with crumbling brickwork, it was the shabbiest in the row. Across the road were two pink gates, just a few feet high, which led into the playground of the village primary school. To the right of Victor's house was a neater property, with window boxes full of flowers and a toddler-sized bike abandoned on the pavement. On the other side were a set of weather-beaten garage doors. The blue paint covering them had faded over time in the sun. A glass frame had been fixed to the other door and inside was an official document – which stated that dangerous wild animals could be kept at this address. As in the UK, it is illegal to keep wild animals as pets in many countries, but you can apply to keep dangerous – non-native – wild animals under a licence scheme. Even with that licence on display, it would have been mad to believe that anything wilder than a domestic cat could be found on this residential street.

But I knew better. At the very least, lions were being kept there.

I'd looked at satellite imagery of this property before I'd left. Stretching out from the rear of Victor's house was a long garden, which ran parallel to the gardens of a group of houses in an adjoining street. Victor's garden ended in a set of rickety old gates opening onto a public street.

Satellite imagery is a fantastic tool. I would use it a lot in my preparation before going undercover. From this eye in the sky, I could look down into Victor's garden and examine what outbuildings and enclosures he had. It's a great way of gathering some initial intelligence to assess what might be going on at a property. At Victor's, I could see a metal training ring, the type used for training lions and tigers in circuses. Switching to 'streetview', I could look over the gates that bordered

4

the street and across to inside the ring. There was a podium of some kind and, lying amongst the patchy grass, I could actually see two lions. Slightly startled, I zoomed out from my screen and back to the street. There, just a few yards away from the lions, I could see two mothers pushing buggies with small children past Victor's gates. How Victor was able to get a 'dangerous wild animals' licence, given the community surrounding his property on every boundary, I'll just never understand.

Peering at the screen from the safety of my home office, I had found that whole scene incredibly surreal but, now, as I stood outside those rickety gates looking down the row of neat family houses, this was clearly a reality. For the children of these homes, there were no fairies at the bottom of their gardens. There were lions.

Standing outside Victor's back gates, all was quiet. I peered through a gap in the gate and into Victor's backyard. Just as the satellite imagery had shown, there was the training ring, all rusty and dominated by tall rye grass that was doing its best to create some savannah amongst an otherwise dusty yard. I couldn't see any lions but the ground inside the training ring was bare, suggesting it was still used.

I banged on the metal gates a few times and shouted, 'Hello!'

A top-floor window opened from the house next door.

'What do you want?' a woman asked.

'I'm looking for Victor,' I said, craning my neck to look back at her.

'He'll be in there somewhere,' she replied. 'Just unravel the chain and go through.'

'What about the lions?' I asked.

'They're all locked up, as are the tigers and bears.'

'What?' I exclaimed.

'Oh yes, you'll find everything in there.'

The expression on her face was very matter-of-fact – as if she got asked that question every day.

I did as I was told. I unravelled the chain and walked through into the main yard. All manner of junk was scattered around this waste ground, including some empty cages and a few trailers strong enough to move big cats in. Beyond the yard were the outbuildings and some chain-link fencing. A wheelbarrow was left in the middle of the track, piled high with big cuts of raw meat. It was a sure sign that Victor must be around and that someone must be hungry.

I called out again but no one answered so I kept moving further into Victor's labyrinth of oddness.

The roar of a male lion is a unique sound and can be heard from up to five miles away but, when it surprises you from just a few feet away, it brings you to your senses in an instant. Shaking off feelings of mild terror, I peered around the fence to see not one but two lions and three tigers pacing small individual cages, each butted up to the other. The cages were just a few yards long and even less wide, so the big cats took up most of the space. In front of these cages was an area of greenery, which I presumed was given over to the cats for occasional exercise. It was empty now. At that moment it almost felt like it was there to taunt the cats. It was a space denied them unless perhaps a trick was performed or their behaviour had been good enough. Amongst the cages, it was a natural space – the tiniest of territories – but it was controlled by man, not the king of the jungle.

Lions are unique in that they are the only cats to live in social groups. Together, they will defend territories of up to 400 square km (154 square miles) of grasslands, scrub or open woodlands.

Here, the cats' enclosures were barren, aside from a mean sprinkling of sawdust scattered over the concrete. A few small logs had been tossed in as a pathetic attempt to make it more exciting but not every cat had access to a log. It was a pitiful way to live for such majestic animals and I wondered what they'd been through before ending up here. Exactly how much of their thirty-year lifespans would have been spent like this?

I took my camera out from the inside of my jacket. Apart from the big cats bellowing out notes of sadness, there were still no human sounds to be heard, so I began documenting their behaviour with my camera. As I filmed, memories of other investigations surfaced when I had been filming animals kept in cages. Whether wild or domesticated, the stereotypical conduct of animals, when they carry out strange repetitive behaviours on a never-ending loop, is always on show in cage systems, and here was no different.

Beyond these enclosures were other caged-off areas so, after a few minutes of recording, I made my way towards them, stopping to film if the chance allowed. I passed by a llama with a missing ear, a wolf that peered out of a den set into an earthy slope and the saddest-looking monkey you could ever imagine. Hunched over in his cage and sitting alone on a tree branch, he looked like the world rested on his shoulders. His watery eyes stared out blankly towards a small copse of trees and would not be drawn to my own.

Next came an old black bear, with patches of bare skin running across her body, which were red raw from constant rubbing against the bars. Then a male lion slumped in the corner of a heavily fortified cage. Alone and with puffed-up eyes, he didn't register my movement. Mangy fur hung in tatters from his neck. People, not life, had beaten it. He was done and I sensed he wished for an end to all this.

It seemed that Victor ran a prison for wildlife, hidden from view, smack bang in suburbia. It was a sad and terrifying place, where animals came to die. I had heard talk of this place also being a retirement home for ex-performers, but it felt more like an asylum – a place where animals were forgotten, driven first to insanity, and then pushed slowly into their graves.

By now I'd reached the back of the house. An old man bent over a spade was in the backyard, as yet unaware of my presence. With silvery grey hair, a moth-eaten, brown jumper and a patched-up pair of dark trousers, Victor didn't strike me as the magnificent lion tamer who would wow crowds in a whirlwind of sequins. Instead, he looked more like his captives.

'Hello, Victor,' I said.

The old man peered up slowly and nodded back at me.

'Can you help me become a lion tamer?' I asked him straight out and before he had a chance to ask me why I was in his garden.

'I'm told you're the main man and I want to become the best, so will you be my mentor?'

Victor perked up and replied, 'Well, you better come inside then.'

So that's what I did.

Inside, Victor's house was a treasure trove of circus memorabilia. Photos in tatty frames hung at odd angles from every wall. Lion cubs, cushioned amongst burly arms, took pride of place, as did tigers sitting obediently on plinths under the canopy of the big top. It was clear to me that Victor had once been a celebrated and revered man in the big-cat-taming community and it did not take him long to tell me this in his own words. He was proud of his achievements.

'I've been involved with circuses for more than fifty years and trained hundreds of animals to perform… too many to remember,' said Victor.

Not wanting to interrupt, I let Victor hold forth at length about his life in the circus. As he showed off each picture, I sat sipping a cup of tasteless coffee.

Victor explained that he started out in circus life by working behind the scenes. Whenever he could, he would watch the showmen tame the lions backstage and then perform to packed-out audiences.

'Over the years, I earned my own way to the top job,' he told me proudly. 'I became the main draw with my own troupe of lions; I was in popular demand.'

Victor had been a lion tamer for a big-name circus that was always on the road. For him, life was good. For the animals, I suspected, less so.

He was now an old man but, as I listened to him, it was clear he was still an integral cog in the breeding machines that supply the circuses with their exotic animals.

'Are any of the animals here for breeding, Victor?' I asked.

'Oh yes, I have lions and tigers here that I use to breed from, though I'd never breed a liger from them. They are crazy.'

Half-male lion, half-female tiger, ligers were gaining in popularity for those circuses still peddling animals as the star attraction. Usually beige with pale brown stripes, they are beautiful, but an oddity only the circus could dream up as they fight for their survival against a public losing interest with the novelty of the circus. As with the tigon (the offspring of a female lion and a male tiger), the liger exists only in captivity because their habitats don't overlap in the wild.

'Let me show you something.' Victor had leaned forward and dropped his voice.

'OK,' I said, not quite knowing where this was going.

'Come with me.'

I followed Victor out of the kitchen and into the backyard. We went past all those pitiful souls I'd already seen, to another pen set slightly back from the others. The lower section was made of a concrete block with wire mesh set on top of that. Inside was a concrete base with a little door in a nearside corner. In the far corner, two young lion cubs were vying for a crack in the wall in which to hide from us. Spitting and snarling, they jostled over the space, while somehow looking for reassurance from each other that everything was going to be OK. They were terrified and they were young; too young to be alone together in this woeful space.

In those moments, I'd switched on my covert camera. With Victor's attention temporarily drawn to a chink in the fence that needed repairing, he suspected nothing.

'They are two months old. I will train them and then they will be sold to the circus. At fifteen months old, they will be ready to perform in public.'

'How old are they when you start the training process?' I asked.

'I begin when they are seven months old.'

I looked at the two cubs. I imagined what their life might be like. They had already been born into a cage and taken away from their mother after just a few weeks. Soon their natural instincts and behaviours would be forced out of them, so they could go on to perform pointless tricks in front of unquestioning audiences. Outside of performances, they would remain in a cage, they would travel in a cage between shows, and their lives would end in a cage at a place like Victor's. Thirty years must be a long time for a lion not to behave like a lion.

Over the next few months, and with the help of Victor's contacts diary, I made a few short trips back across the Channel to other set-ups comparable to Victor's. During that time I saw more lions born into the circus life, and other cubs die in their cage at their mother's side before they could be taken away. Perhaps these were the lucky ones.

I was told how the big cats 'have to know their job'. I heard how they were 'not nice animals, not at all... not one is a good one'. There were few words of affection for the animals, nor much sentiment shown to those retirees that languished in solitary confinement. There was a show but it was always about the showmen – the lion tamers – they were the greatest act on earth.

Things came to an abrupt halt at Victor's in the weirdest of circumstances. One of the lion cub brothers had already gone. Victor had mumbled something about a park in Italy but wouldn't go into details. The other brother, now alone, had also been reserved. He would be going to a big-name circus in Germany in another couple of months but Victor would not be training it. He didn't say why. Aside from those two cubs, there were now three others but they were still far too young to begin training.

Despite the absence of suitable cubs, Victor had decided he was going to show me his training methods. He said I would have to play the part of the lion, for now.

I wasn't quite prepared for what that meant but, given there were no animals to train right now, I could still learn a lot from documenting the process Victor used to train his big cats. So, that's how I found myself kneeling on all fours on top of a stool in the centre of the training ring, while Victor prowled around the perimeter ferociously roaring commands at me. I really hadn't a clue what he was asking me to do but he had transformed into 'The Fearless Lion Trainer' so I stayed put.

He walked with a wooden baton at his side. About the length of a baseball bat, he kept it low to the ground as he padded his way purposefully around the ring. At the end was a small metal claw, which I hadn't noticed initially, but I assumed he'd made it himself. I suspected it wasn't the sort of instrument you'd buy over-the-counter. I started to feel uneasy. I was meant to be the lion, but I felt like the one being hunted – by a pensioner – as he circled his prey, with his own set of claws.

Victor had previously explained the training ring was round so the trainer could dominate while the big cat never felt cornered. Well, Victor, I felt cornered even in the roundest of spaces.

In the end, it wasn't I or Victor who brought this surreal experience to a close. It was a local policeman. I was the first to see the gate open. The last thing I expected was a policeman and, judging by his face, the sight of me kneeling on all fours on a stool while an old man shouted and circled me with a weapon was the last thing he expected.

First, I watched his eyes widen and then his jaw drop as he took in the scene. Nothing was said for a few seconds. I glanced at Victor. Now silent, Victor stared at me, then at the policeman, who looked at me, then at Victor, who had dropped his baton. The policeman glanced at me again. I looked at the ground, wishing it would open up and swallow me.

'Victor, could I speak with you,' the policeman finally said.

Victor nodded. He seemed embarrassed.

That moment felt like a good time to take the weight off my knees and knuckles. Life as a lion was tough on the joints. I eased out of my stance and sat down awkwardly on the stool, like a small child. I nodded at the policeman when I was in a comfortable position as if to say, 'OK, I'm fine. What happens next?'

The policeman was still weighing up the scene as Victor arrived by his side. Then he opened his notepad and began scribbling in it while Victor spoke quietly back to him.

For some reason, I was not asked to participate in the subsequent conversation between Victor and the policeman. Perhaps this was a matter that could only be dealt with between two parties known to each other in the village? I was glad as I didn't want to try and explain what had happened here.

After the policeman left, Victor walked past me and back to the house without saying a word.

While I never got the full story, it seemed an onlooker had alerted the police to this strange spectacle, perhaps thinking some kind of assault on me would take place. After that, Victor sent me away. He became distant and did not return my calls. My training had ended before it had really got started and part of me was glad. It was an upsetting experience to see how circus animals at Victor's were being bred and retired into captivity. So, having documented on camera both the beginning and the end of a circus animal's life, I moved on to filling the gap in between – life at the circus itself.

***

For the next few weeks, I avoided direct contact with circus people. I wasn't keen to be told to sit on a stool and roar like a lion if that was the first step you had to undergo to become a lion tamer. Instead, I watched the goings-on at various circuses – across Europe and the UK – from a greater distance.

I found locations where I could film the animals unnoticed. Rooftops that overlooked the 'beast wagons', through the tinted rear windows of a small delivery van or, at one British circus, draped in a camouflage (camo) cape hidden in a hedgerow near the cages. The latter option was my least favourite. I had to get into the hedgerow before dawn and not leave until darkness had fallen so I wouldn't be noticed.

Once in the dense hedge, I would quietly cut away some of the larger branches, using my Swiss army knife to create a place to sit. Only then would I clear the small branches to open up a gap, through which I could film unobscured. It would take me thirty minutes to get set up and I had to be finished before the first workers started their shift.

I spent a number of long days in that hedge and it proved

useful in documenting the many hours animals would remain caged or tethered, when not performing in the ring. I watched tigers pacing their cages over and over for hours at a time. This was their downtime, a period meant for resting but, to me, they never really looked at ease. I also spent hours filming the elephants and became familiar with the little 'clinking' noise that accompanied the slightest of foot shuffles. Electric fences ran around their tents but the metal chains around their feet were the first line of defence the circus took to ensure they never broke free. The clinking of chains was a constant reminder that the elephants were not here of their own free will. From my hidden position, just a few yards away, I watched these majestic animals sway from side to side or roll a stick up and down their trunk as if making a cigarette. These behaviours were routine and deeply entrenched – the animals' only escape from the frustration and boredom of their lives.

My hedgerow habit came to an abrupt end when, one sunny afternoon, I heard a conversation between two circus workers.

'Sergei, it's your turn to cut the hedge. The elephants need some branches.'

'Yes, I have the chainsaw. I'll do it now,' came the swift response from Sergei.

Aside from brushing the odd mosquito away from my nose, I hadn't had too many distractions until now. I braced myself ready for the worker to come up to the hedge but wasn't too worried as I was very well hidden and a few branches wouldn't give away my position. My mood changed when I heard the chainsaw start up. In came the teeth of a metal tiger, slashing wildly at the hawthorn. Twigs were flying into my face and, when I saw the hairy arms of Sergei jerking the machine deeper into the brush, just inches above my head, enough was enough. I grabbed my camera bag and made a run for it. As I did so, my camo cape snagged on a branch and I exited the hedge with only half of it left flailing around my waist. I stumbled out onto the footpath in front of a family of four, said a brief 'hello' and was gone. Although I heard the chainsaw cut out and someone shouting in the distance I was intent on not getting caught, so stopped for no one as I hastily returned to my van.

After that incident, I switched to a backstage approach where I would go over the fence and walk freely amongst the animal accommodation at first light when the curtains of the workers' caravans were still drawn. Working like this gave me the freedom I needed to see how animals spent the twenty-three hours of any given day when they weren't performing. At one French circus, I was stopped in my tracks by a splashing noise that came from the back of a small van. A series of water pumps and hoses ran to and from it. All was quiet in the caravan next to it, so I walked up to the van ramp and opened the door. Beyond the door was a set of metal railings and behind that, in a pool not much bigger than a bathtub, were two large sea lions.

I'd seen sea lions whilst surfing in California and they made full use of the waves, gracefully riding them towards the shore before swimming back out to do the same again with the next set of waves. Just as I did, they clearly enjoyed riding waves because it was fun. They didn't have to do this for their survival; they chose to do it.

Looking at this pair, it was hard to imagine the speed and grace at which they could swim if just given the freedom to do so. With twitching whiskers and those beautiful, big, dark eyes, they looked at me and then snorted and splashed as much of the water they could at me from their miniature ocean. I quickly took some pictures and then shut the door before the noise would wake someone up.

Later that day I watched the sea lions being led from their

bathtub to the performance area. They walked one behind the other much like ducks waddling together. The worker ushered them along from the rear. Inside the garish canvas tent, they balanced beach balls on their noises and smacked their flippers together to cue up their audience for applause. Thirty minutes later and from a safe distance, I followed their journey back to the lorry, recording them shuffle up the ramp and bellyflop back into the bathtub. I hit the stop button after the worker slammed the door behind them.

I kept working like this for a couple of weeks until a circus worker in a French coastal resort discovered me hidden down the side of one of the tents. I was crouched down between two trailers and had been waiting patiently for the elephants to be unloaded from their trailer when he suddenly appeared in my viewfinder. I started getting my excuse ready but it wasn't looking good for me. He could see several cameras dangling around my neck and I'd walked past a number of 'no photography' signs to get this far. Tall and with sleeves rolled up, he looked pretty menacing as he walked towards me. I was sure it was only a matter of time before he called in the strongman to help rough me up a bit. Maybe they would throw me to the lions. Christ, what was he going to do?

'You want a good time,' he said as he pulled his trouser zipper down, quickly followed by his trousers and underpants. That was the last thing I expected. I'd never heard of the strip act before at the circus.

'What the hell are you doing? And no, I don't!'

As he continued to expose himself to me, three elephants were unloaded behind him, out of view of my camera.

I turned tail and ran, but not before I'd shouted a few obscenities back at the worst act in the circus.

A little traumatised from that experience, I began to wrap things up for this project.

I spent the last few days of this assignment trying to get in with more lion tamers and trainers who provided big cats to the film industry. I had a list of further names that Victor had recommended I should try approaching. While some were potentially interested in training me as an animal handler, I sensed the curtains were coming down on my act. Things were getting more difficult. I was still getting into areas off-limits to the public, and gathering hours of footage to evidence the deplorable living conditions and the scandalous performances these animals were put through each day, but I hadn't been able to film training.

I felt that not being born into a circus family was a huge disadvantage for this project. They trust their own and, while trust could be earned, it would take significant time to find a way inside the secretive training circles of Europe's big-cat tamers.

Thankfully, I don't think there are many people who are planning careers as a lion or tiger tamer. The future success of any animal circus relies on the next generation of circus families wanting to maintain a dying tradition, a public that's prepared to part with its money to watch these animals perform, and a legislation that fails to enforce the national bans coming into force around the world. Twenty-six countries have now banned animal circuses, and many others are preparing legislation to make them illegal.[1] Circuses of the future will find it difficult to remain viable so long as animals remain a part of their plans.

1. https://www.peta.org.uk/blog/these-26-countries-that-have-banned-wild-animal-circuses-are-making-england-look-really-bad/

Bright Eyes

At the bottom of the supermarket trolley were a bunch of baby rabbits. As white as snow and with ruby-red eyes, they sat motionless.

Pushing the trolley was Claudia.

She must have been in her early seventies and had tightly curled silver hair. She moved effortlessly through the aisles as she grabbed the baby rabbits from the trolley and tossed them by the scruff of their necks up into empty cages.

When a cage had been filled with six rabbits, she'd slam the door firmly shut and begin the process again at the next cage.

At the end of each aisle, she would stop to top up the trolley with more baby rabbits who had been crammed into neatly stacked crates by her colleagues.

I stood at the end of one of the aisles, posing as a potential rabbit factory owner. As she passed me, she acknowledged my presence with the slightest of nods.

I was struck by the familiarity of the scene as I looked back down the aisle, which now sparkled with hundreds of bright eyes. It was a factory farm, but it felt more like a supermarket. The product was visible on the shelf and, though not yet canned, the rabbits were already behind metal. The artificial lighting, suspended underneath a metal canopy, felt oddly familiar too.

That nod from Claudia was the only communication I was to have with her but, over the next few weeks, I met more women running their own rabbit factory farms in Italy. This was a country with thousands of rabbit farms and I'd discovered that women were vital components in keeping them ticking over. Until now, I'd rarely come across women running factory farms or as central figures in their management. But in this country, and in this industry, things were different. Women not only managed rabbit farms in Italy, they owned them too.

Promoted as healthy, rabbit meat is produced by an industry that confines more rabbits than egg-laying hens in cages across the European Union, yet hardly anyone I knew had heard of rabbit farming or even considered rabbit to be a farmed animal. It was going to take an investigation to expose this industry. Alongside France and Spain, Italy was one of the key producers, so I began my assignment there, high up in the hills.

I found Claudia's farm on a narrow, winding road. The area was dense with trees. The prickly fruits of sweet chestnuts had begun to fall onto the road and I could hear them snagging in my tyre treads on the drive up.

The farm was set back from the road. A couple of tatty vans were parked up in a courtyard and, beyond them, stood a traditional farmhouse guarded by tall cypress trees. The farmhouse must have been grand at one time but now the ochre paint was peeling badly from the walls, and the climbing plants running around the door were brittle and lifeless.

Before announcing my arrival to Claudia or anyone else at the farm, I took some time to look around unescorted, on my own terms. I parked my car out of sight, gathered my camera equipment and walked through some woodland towards a group of sheds that were on the fringe of the property. Following my own protocol of being opportunistic but not reckless, I made a beeline for the shed furthest from the farmhouse. Waiting for a few minutes to be sure no one was close by, I ran across the last bit of open ground to the shed.

The shed was around ninety yards long, tin-roofed and scruffy. Cautiously, I peeked my head around the entrance. There were no workers present, so I entered.

Filming these rabbits wasn't straightforward. The air was thick with flies. Large bluebottles with their sticky feet made themselves at home on my camera's lens and across its casing. I tried swiping them off with my hand but they were back in seconds and in greater numbers. Looking beyond the flies, it was clear what made that shed so attractive for them: rabbit corpses. In various stages of decay, they were scattered across the aisle, just a few feet below the caged rabbits.

Setting off down the aisle, I picked my way over the bodies until I reached the far end of the shed. The trail of suffering did not end there. It had leached out into the open. Parked up, just back from the door was a mini-tractor. Its front loader, pointed towards the ground, contained more dead rabbits. Their rigid, rotting bodies made it obvious they had been dead for some time. While I was used to seeing animals succumbing to the confines of cage systems, I was slightly taken aback by the sheer quantity of dead rabbits at this farm, and how they had been left out to rot amongst the living.

I turned back to the shed, intent on gathering as much evidence as I could from this farm.

Gusts of wind were now swooshing through the open doors, picking clumps of fur off the floor and swirling them through the building. They danced their way up to the eaves of the roof before descending gently like snowflakes. Bonding with the dust, they coated all the machinery, the feedlines, the ventilation fans and strips of artificial lighting.

Fortunately, the wind had cleared the flies away, so I could finally focus on the living and not the dead. Split across the aisle were two rows of double-tiered cages, stuffed full of rabbits. Youngsters, they were being fattened for their meat. The industry locks them in cages typically for around seventy-five days so they can gain weight before slaughter.[1] Three rabbits were sharing a cage but the space was so cramped they sat with their bodies slumped over one another. Their fur bulged out through the wire mesh seeking escape from such a tiny space.

1. https://www.ciwf.org.uk/farm-animals/rabbits/rabbit-welfare/

In the wild rabbits have a strong drive to run, socialise, play, graze on grass and, perhaps most importantly, burrow to create a space where they can feel safe. These burrows – or warrens – can be 3 m (just over 3 yd) deep, covering a large area with many entrances, and are made up of interconnecting tunnels containing living quarters, nesting areas, bolt runs and emergency exits. If ever there was a place that a rabbit would choose not to be, based on those natural instincts, it would probably be here.

Most of the rabbits in that factory farm had white fur but there was also a smattering of jet-black rabbits. With their dark eyes, they were very beautiful. They reminded me of Inlé, the black spirit-rabbit from *Watership Down*. Inlé took rabbits away at their predestined times of death. Not unlike that character, these black rabbits were surrounded by death, disease and sadness all within the confines of a warren made from stone and mesh.

As usual, I was trying to suppress the knowledge that I could be caught at any moment. While it was a risk I was prepared to take, ending up on the wrong side of the law is unsettling and can have repercussions for your personal life. I prepare well for assignments to minimise those risks but I wouldn't be human if I didn't feel nervous in a place I wasn't meant to be in. To prevent nerves spilling over into something physical, like camera shake, I find coping mechanisms to help keep them in check.

On that day my coping mechanism was to look deep into the eyes of these black rabbits, beyond my own reflection, to a place where I could imagine them as a loved companion animal, hopping happily around a garden with their friends between tasty servings of green leaves; or as wild beings crouched at the base of a hedgerow surrounded by succulent grasses. This was the way our family cared for our rescued rabbits when I was a child. They lived contentedly in a cosy barn alongside the other animals we had rescued or who were passing through on their way to a forever home – chickens, ducks, turkeys. They even had their own natural burrow – they love nothing more than to dig – and I vividly remember rushing home from school so I could see them pop up or hop down into that safe place. We were once given a young unwanted female called, somewhat uncreatively, Doe and, as soon as we released her into our garden, she set right to the task of constructing the perfect home. She chose a site under a bank of bamboo. I was fascinated by how furiously she worked, digging and carrying nesting materials for hours at a time. One day I came home from school to see a tiny white rabbit poking its nose out of Doe's burrow. We didn't have any white rabbits so it was at that point it became clear what had been going on. Doe was working hard to dig the perfect burrow because she was preparing to give birth. 'In another life…', for these rabbits, too, I hoped.

I felt the temptation to free some of them, but I had to resist it. I'd been tested many times like this and, while there have been moments when I have been able to free animals from the misery of their lives on a factory farm, it's not been during an undercover assignment. The risk of getting caught is too high. To release one or two animals at the expense of telling the story of tens of thousands would, in this situation, be a less effective strategy for helping to bring factory farming to an end.

Despite their cuteness, the rabbits here were most definitely not loved pets, nor were they wild rabbits captured and reared on for meat. They had been specifically bred to live this way. This was factory farming at its worst, a cruel secret hidden from the average consumer. Rabbits are produced in similar conditions to the cage-based rearing systems used for egg-laying hens but without the same public debate. I was hoping this investigative assignment could spark some controversy and provide some real home truths to better inform the public.

***

Having had valuable time undetected on the farm, I left the shed and sought out the owner. I found Claudia in the main shed, closest to the farmhouse. As with many of my investigations, I'd prepared a cover story and brushed up on my Italian, a language I loved studying. For this assignment my cover story was that I planned to start a rabbit farm back home and that I was in Italy to learn what I could from those more experienced than me.

Claudia bought my cover story but was reluctant to speak with me. She was busy 'restocking the shelves' with rabbits, so it fell to her nephew, Giancarlo, to fill in the gaps about how this farm was run.

Giancarlo started by telling me about the history of the farm, but we were stood next to a bucket full of dead rabbits and I wanted to get straight to the point about the mortalities.

'There are a lot of dead rabbits here, Giancarlo. Why is that?'

'This industry suffers from higher mortalities than other livestock farming sectors,' he said. 'We spend twenty-five thousand euros per year on antibiotics and vaccines at this farm. Rabbits are very delicate.'

'Delicate?' I'd heard that word before during my pre-investigation research. I'd spoken with Cesare, an Italian farmer, who had given up farming rabbits quite recently, though sadly not for welfare reasons. During our conversations, he had also described rabbits as being, 'very delicate, as they normally would be when free, but they get worse when put in a cage and when given food that is not natural for them'.

While the industry hides, its farmers weren't hiding the problems they faced in trying to farm rabbits. Both existing and former farmers talked openly about the challenges of fitting these creatures into the cage culture of modern-day agriculture.

Giancarlo had moved on to talk about the feed that they give the rabbits. As he spoke, I looked around the warehouse. There was no sign of any natural feed here. Nothing green or high fibre, which a rabbit would want to forage on in the wild; just processed feed coming out of sacks in pellet form and being pushed automatically to each cage via a freeway of feedlines running overhead. With huge stockpiles of feed stacked up at the back of the warehouse, it seemed there was never any variety in their diet.

A piercing scream then resonated across the room. Behind Giancarlo, I could see Claudia grappling with a large doe – a female rabbit. The sound of a rabbit vocalising like that is chilling and even Giancarlo seemed uneasy about it, so he attempted to fill the gap in our conversation with words.

'She is moving the does that haven't got pregnant to new cages.'

Claudia forced the doe into the cage and was preparing to repeat the procedure with other failed would-be mothers. Clearly terrified, they desperately hopped and scrambled over each other at the bottom of Claudia's trolley.

'They will be re-inseminated again,' Giancarlo said. 'Would you like to see that?'

I really didn't want to see that process but it would be valuable for the project to document such a regular and invasive procedure, so nodded in agreement.

Together we walked to another shed, where, as he put it, the 'breeding' was done. Giancarlo looked at his watch and apologised for having to leave me for something more pressing. He left me, as he detailed, in the 'capable hands' of one of their workers, who was bent over a trolley preparing a set of torturous-looking utensils.

Luca, the worker undertaking the procedure, shook my hand and then directed me to scrub up, making it clear he wanted me to cover up my top half with the lab coat and the face mask that he'd thrust in my hand. Like me, he also wore just a jacket and face mask but, poking out from beneath his coat, were board shorts, socks and sandals. Topped off with a baseball cap, he looked like a tourist on a cheap beach holiday.

Inside the breeding unit were 500 does. Some were already mothering litters, others were pregnant or about to become pregnant. There were also six bucks – male rabbits. They were kept alone in cages and used exclusively for reproduction. If in good health, they can live eight years or more but, in a cage, that's unlikely. As they are social animals, putting a rabbit in solitary confinement exacerbates abnormal behaviours and is just another example of how animals in factory farms fit a system that's built for profit, not for the needs of the animal.

I watched Luca grab a buck from a cage and thrust it on top of a doe who sat frozen in panic. While keeping one hand pinned down on the buck he used his other hand to put a receptacle in between the buck and the doe to catch the semen. Seconds later, clutching the buck by the scruff of his neck, he thrust him back in his cage and slammed the door shut.

I peered in at the pitiful doe and noticed her fur was patchy and worn in places.

'Luca, why's her fur so patchy?' I asked.

'I use her just for the bucks, they can be rough when they think they're mating.'

Over and over again she would be used like this. I felt incredibly sad at that moment, knowing her sole purpose in life was to endure this 'procedure'.

Luca returned to his grubby little office. He examined the

semen under a microscope and then turned to me with a smile and the thumbs-up gesture to say he was happy with what he'd collected.

'I have forty does to inseminate – let's go.'

He added the semen to tubes in a cool box, which had already been set up on the metal trolley. Alongside it was a syringe, some plastic tubes, some sprays and a vaccination gun. I followed him wheeling it back into the breeding unit at a great pace. Then I took a deep breath as the door slid back.

The next forty-five minutes was painful viewing for me, but nothing compared to what the animals endured. Though I didn't show it, I felt distressed documenting that process with my covert camera. Luca was like a machine, yanking does from their cages, pinning them down and raising their tails up, while simultaneously pushing the plastic tube inside of them. A syringe then fired the semen into the tube. The whole process took around thirty seconds for each doe.

I followed Luca down the line. I asked him if I could film and he was fine with it so, while my covert camera was running, I used another camera with him openly, to allow me more control over what I captured.

The first ten rabbits Luca inseminated showed no external signs of sickness or injury. The next batch, however, were not in a good way.

Conjunctivitis was causing their eyes to weep and some were completely crusted over, almost to the point where they were blind in one eye. Others had serious head tilts, caused by a parasitic infection to the ear. They were unable to raise their heads up normally. Instead, their heads would hang low; one eye pointing up to the ceiling, the other down to the shit-coated floor. They were all mothers, nursing young, but they were also breeding machines so no time was wasted in getting them pregnant again. Female animals, as the producers of the next generation, endure some of the very worst abuses in factory farming.

Tiny baby rabbits – or kits – that nuzzled their mothers scattered as Luca's hand came down swiftly into each cage – all except for one, which lay dead in a corner of the cage. 'Staying Alive' by the Bee Gees was playing on the radio.

'There is a dead one in the cage, Luca,' I said.

'Yes, that's normal. Sometimes one or two will die during the rearing process. This doe actually gave birth to fifteen rabbits but I always cull five at the beginning, so she can manage better.'

I could see how this industry had the highest mortality rates in factory farming but didn't expect that number to include so many healthy animals, which farms weren't prepared to rear.

Luca was approaching the end of the row and decided now was the time to start asking me some questions. I was prepared for that, so calmly answered them without any wavering.

'So you're going to make your own rabbit farm in Britain, yes?'

'That's right,' I said.

'How many will you have?'

'Two sheds with a small on-site slaughterhouse, capable of slaughtering two-and-a-half thousand rabbits per week. I'm also considering breeding rabbits to supply to the research industry. I can make nine hundred per cent more profit per rabbit that way than I can for a meat rabbit.'

'Really.' Luca nodded. I took that to mean I had his approval.

I always prepared thoroughly when using a cover story to gain access to animal breeding facilities. I knew how much things cost and sold for, where I could source equipment, who were the main industry players, even the names of a few well-known individuals, whom I made sure to speak with before starting out on a project. Then I could name-drop to help gain some credibility if I sensed my story wasn't being bought.

'You'll probably need some help to do this,' Luca said as he packed away his insemination tubes.

'My wife normally helps me...' he paused for a moment as he wiped the last insemination tube clean, 'but she's pregnant right now.'

Back in Luca's office, I thanked him for his time while I put my lab coat and mask in the wash bin. Standing there, beach-ready in his board shorts, he said, 'You'll know how to do this when you start your farm now.'

I nodded and, as I left, glanced at his outfit and wished him a happy holiday.

He looked perplexed but thanked me anyway.

***

As part of any investigative factory farm project, I look to get evidence from as many factory farms as I can. It's much harder for officials or industry bodies to refute footage if it comes from more than one farm. From a campaigning perspective, you also get to learn so much about an industry from the inside and that can be a big advantage in preparing a campaign challenge against an industry or bad practice.

So, after Claudia's farm, I travelled a few hundred miles south to an area with more rabbit factory farms. Close to some glitzy beach resorts on the Adriatic coast, I'd deemed this spot far enough away from the previous location that factory farmers wouldn't talk amongst themselves about a strange foreigner asking too many questions about rabbit farming.

I first heard Martha shouting from an open window of her house on the main road. I was outside her factory farm.

Martha told me to wait there before disappearing from sight. I waved back to let her know I'd understood her.

Just as I'd done at Claudia's farm, I'd already snuck around the back of Martha's farm to film a little through some open windows on the outside of the breeding unit, and I'd also documented some buckets that were close to overflowing with empty medication bottles. The bottles were evidence of this industry's addiction to medication. Without a constant stream of antibiotics and vaccines, this industry would not be viable.

Martha was a tall, wiry woman with a warm smile. She listened intently as I explained my cover story.

'I'm on a fact-finding mission to help me start a rabbit farm back home. Would you mind if I ask you a few questions?'

'Do you want to see inside?' she asked.

'Well, yes, if you don't mind. I don't have an example to look at in the UK, so have come here to learn as much as I can from those in the know.'

'OK, let's talk inside where I can show you both the breeders and the fatteners.'

I followed her into the unit, only stopping to stroke a little cat that I'd already noticed from the shed windows running around beneath the rabbit cages.

Inside, the unit was dirty and dusty. Straightaway, I could see some dead rabbits left out on top of the cages. They were very decomposed. I could understand the cat's thinking better now.

'I've invested three hundred thousand in this unit and the equipment,' Martha said.

She didn't say when that had been but, judging by the state of the place, it wasn't any time recently. Maybe she was thinking of Italian lira, not euros.

She was the owner and had run the farm herself for the past twenty-five years. Occasionally, her family would help out but they had other jobs away from the family farm. She had 700 does, which were producing 20,000 rabbits for slaughter ('fatteners' as she'd called them) every year. That was a lot of work for one person. Perhaps the sheer quantity of work was a contributing factor as to why the farm looked in such poor shape.

I wanted to understand more about why Martha did this work, so asked her outright. Her response surprised me.

'I like animals. But it is important to stay detached from them. I farm them to sell on. I don't want to slaughter them, just to sell them.'

The fact that the person she sold them to immediately killed them didn't seem to enter her perspective. It's difficult for me to accept that factory farmers 'like' animals, given the living conditions they raise them in. I think Martha meant she liked working with them, which is quite different.

Rather than seeing animals as loved companions that we enjoy, respect and treat like family, I think Martha meant she liked having animals around because they provided her with the things that she needed. The rabbits were here to generate an income for her; and, in an otherwise lonely existence, the rabbits were also her only company during long days spent alone.

Likewise, the cat running between the aisles and the duck waddling around the shed exterior were there to carry out a job, rather than because Martha liked them personally. The cat was deterring rodents – attracted to the spilled food and the dead bodies – from venturing inside the unit, while the duck was a cheap alarm system to warn Martha of unannounced visitors. Every animal here had a purpose for Martha.

Despite offering a great deal to their owner, these rabbits were held prisoners in their tiny cells and never received anything in return.

While Martha was very keen to distance herself from the killing process – despite being a cog in that machine – she did tell me exactly where they went to be slaughtered. So, after I'd thanked Martha for her time, that's where I went next.

Like the farms, the slaughterhouse taking Martha's rabbits was run by women and it doubled up as a butcher's shop. It was on the edge of a small town and it had a big glass window that faced onto the street. It was decorated with some of the meat products processed there, mostly rabbits wrapped up in plastic and draped with an Italian flag, but there was also some other meat on display, mainly pigeon and duck.

I noted that the slaughterhouse was small, which usually meant that gaining entry would be less daunting. I also had another ace up my sleeve: I could now name-drop Martha.

Once I mentioned her name, the owners were OK with me watching the slaughter process and guided me out back to the slaughter zone where they left me alone with the workers. It was only 7 a.m., but work was well underway judging by the workers' white aprons, which were heavily streaked with fresh blood.

Three women were working the slaughter line. Two looked like bona fide slaughterhouse workers. They were dressed from head to toe in hygienic workwear: a white jacket, white apron, grey trousers and white boots. The other woman wore a floral dress, the type my grandma wore in the 1970s, and a pair of green Wellington boots. I noticed the varicose veins that navigated her legs.

Luisa was well past retirement age and seemed to be a law unto herself.

'Let the animal die first,' were the first words I heard from Anamaria, her colleague, who was operating the stunning machine that rendered the rabbits unconscious in preparation for their throats to be cut. It seemed the old lady was trying to skin them too quickly after their throats had been cut and had been reprimanded, maybe only because I was there.

Luisa nodded and stepped off a box she'd been standing on to give her the extra height she needed to reach the dead rabbits, which were suspended by their back legs above her from metal hooks. As she stepped down, she stopped and glared at me. I could see her grip tighten around the knife she was holding. She walked over to me, only stopping when she was well inside the comfort zone of my own personal space. As she looked me dead in the eyes, she sliced the knife repeatedly through the air and spoke to me in a menacing tongue. What she had to say sounded as though it came from a much darker place than the atmosphere of this well-lit room. With my back to the wall, there was nowhere I could go.

'She says you're nice and wants to know how old you are,' translated one of the workers, and laughed.

'OK… well, if she's chatting me up, could you ask her to put the knife down first?' I said, trying to make light of the situation.

The old lady smiled a toothless grin.

According to her colleagues, she had been working there for the past thirty years. I got the feeling she appeared when the veterinarian wasn't around and, from what I was told, she wasn't around that often anymore, which the younger women seemed happy about. Without an on-site veterinarian in a slaughterhouse, there is no one who can enforce both animal welfare and food hygiene standards.

While the workers laughed off Luisa's chat-up technique, I noticed a crate full of young rabbits on the floor. It was turned up on its side so the rabbits were toppling onto each other. By European Union (EU) law, these crates should have been kept horizontal on the floor to prevent injuries.

The same legislation also required that animals should not see each other being slaughtered. And yet these rabbits were looking directly at the stunning machine, which, in a few moments, would be sending a surge of electricity through their bodies, shocking them into unconsciousness before their throats would be cut.

It was clear this slaughterhouse was blatantly ignoring welfare laws. As in so many places, the workers held them in disregard, even telling me that the laws were too complicated and exaggerated.

Luisa was back in position on her box as the first of the young rabbits was pulled from the crate by Anamaria. He was a white rabbit with a little black speck on his nose. I watched his head being forced down between the two metal prongs of the stunning device. Cables that had been repaired in places with red electrical tape led up from the power source on the floor. The rabbit's paws shook violently while Anamaria held it down. But, rather than rendering the rabbit unconscious with one swift motion, Anamaria had to repeat the process, forcing his head into the machine again and again before, finally, the rabbit lost consciousness. Then she hung him on the processing line and slit his throat.

Inconsistency would be the word I would use to describe what I saw that day. Some rabbits were stunned quickly and effectively but others were not so fortunate. When stunned ineffectively, the rabbits were repeatedly given searing electric shocks before being rendered unconscious. On more than one occasion, I saw signs of rabbits regaining consciousness whilst bleeding out. I can't imagine how terrifying it must be to wake up with your throat slit and to experience the full agony of bleeding to death – that's if Luisa doesn't also start to skin you alive.

I asked Anamaria about the age of the stunning equipment. She told me the equipment was indeed old and, while that's not always a sign of being obsolete, the patched wires running up to the prongs made me wonder whether that was the reason for the irregular stunning.

I documented one hundred rabbits slaughtered that day. I could sense their fear as they peered out from the crate up to the stunner and beyond to where the carcasses were suspended. The fleshy carcasses were unrecognisable as rabbits – save for the little patches of white fluff left on their paws, which are hacked off last of all – but to other rabbits they would have smelled like their own kind.

As I gazed at the carcasses, I suddenly noticed an anomaly.

A large patch of dark red blood stood out like a fresh tattoo on otherwise pink flesh. It was located on the upper thigh. I pointed it out to Anamaria, who told me it was as a result of a broken leg. The heavy bruising suggested it was sustained while the rabbit was in the crate.

So many farmers told me how delicate rabbits were during this project, which begs the question: why incarcerate them in the first place? Words mean nothing, it's actions that count, and I never saw any workers on these farms treat rabbits like delicate animals or with any kind of compassion or respect. They were routinely tossed from side to side, yanked by the ears or grabbed by their fur right up to the point they lost their life.

In the wild, rabbits normally live out much of their lives underground in warrens, in the company of other rabbits. But in this industry, it's the rabbit farmers that hide underground, keen to keep their cruel systems out of the public spotlight. And for a long time they've done well in keeping the secret that every year 330 million rabbits are reared across the EU for meat and pet food – almost entirely in intensive cage systems.[2] However, change is underway and the footage from my inves-

2. https://www.ciwf.org.uk/farm-animals/rabbits/

tigation formed part of a dossier of evidence which, in 2017, helped convince the European Parliament to vote in favour of putting an end to the use of cages for rabbits farmed for meat. The vote was the first significant step towards securing legislation to outlaw the practice once and for all.[3]

Anamaria had shrugged off the broken leg that rabbit had suffered in the transport crate. But as I left, I looked back and saw her come through the plastic strip curtains separating the unloading area from the slaughter room. She was pushing another crate of rabbits into the room. They were also the wrong way up.

3. https://www.ciwf.org.uk/news/2017/03/monumental-success-for-europes-farmed-rabbits

Spoiled Chickens

Chip's baseball cap looked like it had been welded to his head. I couldn't imagine him leaving home without it. It was beige with an illegible motif, and the peak sat just above rounded glasses. He wore a pale blue-and-white striped shirt, matching dungarees and dirty brown boots. Somehow he reminded me of wallpaper.

He said nothing when Barb greeted me. She looked tired and slightly dishevelled in a brown t-shirt and high-waisted, white trousers. I didn't ask where she was from but her accent sounded more East Coast US than the slower-paced drawls I had become accustomed to in the Deep South. Chip and Barb owned a chicken factory farm, but not for much longer. They wanted out. They were selling up, and that's why I was there, posing as a prospective buyer.

***

Each year more than 9 billion chickens are reared and slaughtered in the USA.[1] That's more than anywhere else in the world.[2] The chicken industry in the USA is a roost ruled by just a handful of giant food corporations.[3] In turn, they contract more than 25,000 farms like Chip and Barb's to grow birds for them. Under these contracts, the 'growers', as they're known, are given chickens, along with a set of requirements for production that they must meet to keep their contracts alive.

And the chickens they're given aren't any old chickens. In fact, all the big producers use what's called a fast-growing breed. These birds have been genetically selected to grow to a huge size in an

1. https://www.nationalchickencouncil.org/about-the-industry/statistics/broiler-chicken-industry-key-facts/
2. https://www.statista.com/statistics/237597/leading-10-countries-worldwide-in-poultry-meat-production-in-2007/
3. https://www.theguardian.com/environment/2019/aug/03/is-the-us-chicken-industry-cheating-its-farmers

incredibly short period of time. In 1950 it took sixteen weeks to get chickens to a 'marketable' age. Now, they go from chick to oven-ready in just seven weeks. And they're cheap. While the shopper makes the savings, the cost to the chickens' welfare is adding up and the government isn't doing what it should to regulate that process. In the USA, there are no federal laws on the welfare of animals used in agriculture.[4] So, I was on a mission to document these animals' lives, though it wasn't going to be easy.

The timing of this assignment had clashed with a new wave of gagging laws aimed at protecting industrial agriculture from organisations that exposed cruelty cases at factory farms. At the time of my arrival, several prominent farming states, including Iowa, Montana and Utah, had passed laws to prevent under-cover activists like myself secretly filming in factory farms.[5] The fear factor they created had begun to have an impact and several campaigning organisations I'd spoken to were limiting their investigations in those states that had passed bills or were likely to do so in the upcoming months. I'd heard rumblings that states in the South were considering such legislation, so to put some distance between myself and this pending legisla-tion, which the media had termed 'ag-gag', I posed as a poten-tial buyer of the farm rather than get a job on a chicken farm, which I felt could have put me at greater risk under this type of law. I knew the chicken industry was on high alert when it came to assessing on-farm job applications but there should be no alarm bells ringing if I approached the owners of a farm directly, especially one that was up for sale. So that's what I did and now I was undercover.

***

4. https://www.britishpoultry.org.uk/identity-cms/wp-content/uploads/2018/05/2016-ADAS-EU-US-comparison.pdf

5. https://www.aspca.org/animal-protection/public-policy/what-ag-gag-legisla-tion

Barb was younger than I had expected. She was a mother to four of the wildest-looking children I had ever seen. I saw them as I drove up the gravel track from the main road: long-haired creatures sitting by tree stumps. All had pale blonde hair and were scratching away at sticks with knife blades.

They glared at me just long enough to make me feel uncomfortable when I pulled up alongside them. Did they know I was wearing a hidden camera? Of course not, I told myself, shrugging off the mild paranoia that can sometimes surface when working like this.

'Are your folks in?' I asked.

One of them leaped off the stump and ran back to the wooden cabin without uttering even a grunt in my direction. The others watched me closely until Barb and Chip arrived.

Though we hadn't met before, I had been in contact with the couple for several months as they tried to sell the farm. I usually spoke with Barb but occasionally got stuck on the phone with Chip's elderly mother who lived with them and found my British accent particularly fascinating. They had advertised their two-shed broiler chicken farm (a broiler is specifically raised for meat production) on a land agent's website. The sales particulars said the farm was also being sold with a four-bedroomed house. It was described as having two bathrooms, a large laundry and a walk-in pantry. I figured the ad made it sound like the ideal buyer would be someone with bad odour and a big appetite.

Estate agents are the same all over when it comes to prose. Calling it a 'house' was a bit of a stretch. A backwoods log cabin was probably a more honest assessment. Not particularly big, but cosy enough inside with a huge fireplace to keep warm through the winter. Part of me would have been very happy living in a simple place like this but a family of seven must have struggled here.

Barb sat me down on a huge leather sofa and we chatted

for quite a while. I knew I'd need to be patient before seeing inside the chicken sheds, so a bit of small talk was going to be required. They talked about the house, the weather and their family. They also hinted that they were a bit behind on the farm upgrades that the chicken company required.

'You'll have to put a bit of cash aside to do some of the upgrades on the farm,' Barb said.

'What kind of upgrades?' I asked.

'Well, the company want thirty to fifty thousand dollars invested in the chicken sheds and the equipment to help modernise the place. You've got to do that to meet your contractual obligations,' she said.

'And you haven't wanted to do that?' I probed.

'No, but we've priced the farm to reflect that,' she hastily added.

An hour of small talk had passed when Barb finally turned to Chip and said, sharply, 'Why don't you show Rich the land?'

Chip nodded, ushered me to the door and took me on a hike of the plot. They owned a huge chunk of woodland and I think we walked nearly all of it over the next few hours.

The wood was quiet and peaceful. It was noon and, with the sun high in the sky, there were no birds to be heard. All I could hear was the noise of our boots shuffling through the leaf litter on the narrow tracks criss-crossing the land. A neat little line of carpenter ants marched the length of a fallen tree. The wood was dense. Tightly bunched and rolling up and down on the steep terrain were the beech trees, their pale bark bouncing sunlight back and forth, helping to add a touch of gloss to their dark green leaves.

Chip was still very reserved so I started asking him about the wildlife living in these woods, hoping to break our conversational stand-off. First, I asked him about copperhead snakes. I'd eavesdropped on some locals talking about them in a roadside café a few days back. I'd learned they like skulking in rotting wood piles and there was a lot of dead wood in here.

'They're here but I don't see them,' said Chip shortly.

'How about foxes?'

I knew these woods would be the ideal habitat for the small grey fox that liked to climb trees with its little hooked claws.

'Don't think so,' said Chip.

It turned out Chip didn't know much about the wild animals on his land unless, that is, you asked him about deer. I'd seen plenty of guns hanging off the wall back in the cabin so I took a chance on Chip being a deer hunter.

'You got any white-tail deer here?'

'Deer?' said Chip, turning to me. His tone had changed completely as I hit on a subject of interest to him.

I'd hit the jackpot. Chip finally opened up. He loved deer. Tracking them, hunting them, killing them, skinning them, mounting their heads on a wall. I'd finally broken the monosyllabic conversation and his pace quickened as he sought out every deer track he could find to share his passion with me. It transpired there were a lot of deer in these woods. Basking in the relief of not having to lead the conversation any longer, my mind wandered while he talked about his hunting expeditions. I imagined buying the property and turning the whole plot into a deer sanctuary.

When we ran out of deer tracks to inspect, Chip suggested we go look at the chicken sheds.

'Can we go back via the house first, Chip? I need to use the restroom.'

What I really meant was I needed to turn my hidden camera on.

'Sure, you go ahead,' he said.

Inside the bathroom, I set about checking the camera and getting it running. I was sweating from the hike through the warm woods and the duct tape that held the wires to my skin had started to wilt.

If the tape came unstuck, the wires would shift. They might hang out the bottom of my shirt and they'd certainly pull the tiny camera, concealed in a shirt buttonhole, out at an awkward angle. Shirt buttons pointing up to the sky are a problem for two reasons: one, I don't need any aerial footage; and two, real buttons don't point up – ever. It's a sure-fire way to get noticed.

Having replaced some of the duct tape, I met up again with Chip outside. We walked towards the sheds and passed by some of the machinery that had come up in our chat earlier – the John Deere tractor with a front loader, the two rundown barns, some electric fencing, barbed wire and a cruster machine.

The cruster machine was used to de-cake the foul chicken litter that quickly builds up in the sheds when there are 50,000 chickens on site at any one time. It was parked up in one of the shabby barns. Pulled by a tractor, it breaks up the old litter and excrement and shunts it into a trailer so it can be removed easily from the sheds when the flocks get changed over. The machine was looking pretty crusty itself.

It had been more than a few hours since I arrived but I could now see the chicken sheds. There were two, tucked well away from public sight. Even from the hill where the cabin was perched, they weren't visible. Yet they were comparable in size to the vast chicken sheds that I'd filmed in Europe, which are often deliberately hidden from public view. There, the placement of factory farms close to communities had led people to consider and challenge the ethics of factory farming. Perhaps learning from that experience, the chicken industry then began building them out of sight, in an attempt, possibly, to keep them out of people's minds.

Barb and Chip's farm was a bit of an anomaly in this region. As I travelled there on the state roads, I'd seen many prominent chicken factory farms. But, as I'd learned from my research, many farming families here had adopted the contract lifestyle. Everyone, it seemed, had a connection to growing chickens, so there was really no need to hide it from your neighbours.

As we approached, I noticed a narrow grassy strip between the sheds. At one end, I could hear a feed truck swooshing grain loudly into one of the shiny aluminium feed-hoppers. I imagined them being employed in some capacity by astronauts for the first moon landings. Somehow, they had ended up here with their stumpy legs and reflective silver coatings. Watching the feed cascading out of the truck, I asked Chip, and Barb who had joined us, what was in it.

'Probably corn,' Barb said. 'I know it's animal protein-free, which the chicken company likes to tell its customers, but it's their secret formula so we don't rightly know.'

'I don't care,' said Chip. 'It's someone else's job to think about that.'

I looked up at the sky. The corrugated tin roofs stretched back 150 m (around 500 ft). The bright, hot sun bounced off them, momentarily blinding me. Each shed had a big double door that could be opened wide enough to get a tractor through. To an outsider, there was no telling who – or what – the sheds contained. Judging by the CCTV camera pointing down over the doors, that's the way they wanted it to stay. Outsiders were not welcome – unless you might be buying the farm.

Like the roof, tin also wiggled its way down the shed sides, only to be interrupted by cooling pads and huge noisy fans that controlled the temperature and extracted foul air from inside. I approached one of the fans to check if I could see all the way inside. I could make out a white mass but the pungent air pouring out quickly moved me along.

Having walked the length of the shed, we returned to the midway point of shed number one. Now Chip ushered me through the door into a small room fitted out with rough-coated sheet board. For such a tiny space, it was chaotic. Alarm systems, phones, notice boards and Walmart bags, which contained the spare parts of a chicken drinker system, were scattered across the office. Looking down on the confusion was a small statue of the Virgin Mary. I'd seen lots of religious icons adorning similar spaces in factory farms. I suspect they're placed to watch over and protect the farmers and their profit margins, though a little part of me wonders whether they're also there to beg forgiveness for what's on the other side of the door.

Looking for evidence that would connect me more to the animals than the fixtures and fittings of the farm, I peered down into a bucket where an empty medication bottle lay. 'AMPRO-LIUM' was written in large letters across the bottle's label. I asked Chip what they used this bottle for and Chip confessed that some of the chickens had gotten sick.

He described how he added the medication to the water system to fight an outbreak of coccidiosis – an infection that can wreak havoc in a flock of chickens. The disease spreads from one bird to another by contact with infected faeces or ingestion of infected tissue. I scanned the notice board to look for anomalies in the data sheets and a set of mortality figures caught my attention. I quickly totted up the deaths – more than 230 in week five of the chickens' seven-week growing period. Chip saw my attention had been drawn to the sheets and hastily explained that this batch, he believed, had arrived here from the hatchery with stomach problems. I started flicking through the mortality sheets from previous batches and saw other periods where mortalities jumped up during the growing period.

Chip chipped in and said, 'You can take those sheets away with you if you like.'

'Thanks, that would be useful,' I said. 'Don't you need them, though, for your records?'

'I never look at the sheets. Maybe it's lazy of me but, if I'm not required to do it, and I'm not, then I just won't mess with it.'

It seemed to me that Chip really didn't care much for his job or his livestock. Chip began reaching for the door, which led to the chickens, so I bundled the sheets into my back pocket and joined him. I directed my chest towards the door, so my concealed camera would get a clear shot of that moment. I also braced myself for the wave of heat and ammonia that I knew would immediately escape the oppressive conditions inside.

As the door opened I darted in front of Chip so I could get unobstructed filming. Perhaps he thought I was rude but I hoped it would be seen more as eagerness from an interested buyer. The shed was longer than a football field. To the front and side of me was a thick carpet of white feathers. These were the residents I'd been wanting to meet and in this shed alone there were nearly 25,000 of them.

'These chickens are just one day away from being slaughtered,' said Chip.

I nodded, although I already knew that. When I had initially contacted Barb about the farm, I had asked many questions about the condition of the building, the equipment and what upgrades the company would be requiring. During those conversations, I casually slipped in a question about how old the birds were. I had planned my visit to coincide with the final days of their lives – when their bodies had been pushed beyond their physical capabilities – which is when the symptoms of abuse and neglect in the modern-day broiler chicken are most visible.

I took a few steps forward into the sea of chickens and then stood still. They had turned their heads towards us when the door opened, possibly sensing danger. But Chip kept on moving through them. He scuffed his boots through the dirty litter just as he had done in the woodland but, instead of leaves, he was also kicking birds out of his way. If this was a daily occurrence, then I could see why the birds might be stressed by the arrival of people. The floor moved like storm-driven whitecaps raging far out to sea as the birds flocked together to escape the centre of the storm – Chip's boots. In the same way as a swell moves, these birds ruffled their feathers in unison.

Straightaway, I made some references to the roof and the feedlines. They were dusty and coated in cobwebs. I couldn't be seen to focus solely on the chickens initially. As Chip answered, I turned my body slowly through 180 degrees to capture the scene across the full length of the space.

Barb appeared at the door to call Chip over for a signature. While they were distracted, I took my chance to crouch down and focus in closer on individual birds. I knew from the joys of keeping my own rescued chickens how individualistic they can be but in here it was hard to pick up any differences between them. This wasn't helped by their splayed legs. Buckling under their heaving chests, the birds staggered left and right like boxers fighting to stay on their feet after a series of thundering blows. They were all carrying too much weight for their skeletons, but that's what the industry has spent years of genetic tinkering on. A tap on my shoulder made me jump.

'I think this feeder's blocked,' I told Chip before he had a chance to ask me why I was crouching.

'Really?' Chip said.

He bent down to look and a few more chickens dragged themselves out of harm's way.

As Chip began to examine the feeder, I decided to confront him about the chickens with the most noticeable leg problems.

'What's up with those birds, Chip?'

'Sometimes they have bad legs… I don't know why.'

Barb joined in. 'They get real heavy, especially the "roasters", which get reared to three months or more, but these birds are generally pretty big.'

It seemed that Barb and Chip were waiting for me to respond. I said nothing, knowing that if you stay silent long enough, most people will break the silence themselves without any need to ask more probing questions.

'Sometimes they'll have a heart attack, or they'll get flipped over on their backs and die not being able to right themselves,' Barb added.

We were all now staring at one bird that wasn't well enough to drag itself away from us. It was a pitiful sight.

'He'll make it through another day,' said Chip.

Chip turned away and ushered me away. There was an obvious need to end this bird's suffering, but Chip was seeing a bird coated in dollar bills, not feathers. I couldn't let my concern show, but the data sheets were starting to make sense now. I followed them into the next section of the shed in silence.

'These are the special ones,' Barb then said proudly. Her hands were outstretched, as if she was talking about all the chickens on her farm.

'Special ones?' I asked.

Chip casually tossed two dead chickens he'd picked out from the masses to the side of the shed.

'Yep, they're all natural, animal protein-free, no antibiotics. You can't buy them locally – only in the big town stores.'

I struggled to see how these chickens, which were essentially confined in a huge warehouse and unable to stand without great difficulty, could ever be seen as 'natural' to most consumers, yet it seemed they were being sold as a premium product. Chip then mentioned a couple of towns where they were

sold and explained that the whole bird would be packaged up
and labelled as 'proudly raised by a family farm'.

'I never saw one with our actual name on it, but I don't really
care,' Chip said before he returned to tossing dead chickens
towards buckets placed at the side of the sheds.

He was never going to be a basketball player, I thought, as
another chicken missed the bucket by a country mile and thud-
ded into the wall.

'There's so many chickens in here, you can easily walk over
a dead one,' Chip said nonchalantly.

I'd walked over four like that just catching up with him. He
hadn't noticed them.

'How often should I check on the birds?' I asked.

'A couple of times a day. I do it after breakfast, then you can
go fishing or into town.'

I imagined Chip peering briefly in the shed at all the thousands of desperate chickens every day before heading off to a
lake to stare for hours at a small float bobbing on the surface of
a lake.

By now our earlier talk of upgrades, holes being patched up
and the costs of heating fuel had been forgotten. I felt Barb and
Chip were comfortable with me and the line of questioning I
was taking. It felt more like a conversation now than a sales
pitch and the subject was the chickens.

'These birds have the life,' said Barb.

'The life?' I asked.

'Yeah, you know some of these environmentalist people
wanna complain about it, but you know these birds have the
life.'

Chip corrected Barb, 'You mean the animal rights people.'

He didn't know it but he meant people like me. I gestured
for them to continue.

'They're not out scouring around for food, you know,' Barb added. 'It's all laid on.'

I thought about how my chickens back home excitedly leave their straw-lined nest boxes each morning for the daily bug chase around the garden, even though there's always a trough of food they could eat more easily.

Barb continued, 'We don't want to mistreat these birds. We keep them comfortable. They eat when they want to, they drink when they want to, they sit down when they want to. They're not out looking around for food all over the place. They've got good feed, so you know they really do have the life.'

'Until it's time to kill them,' chimed in Chip.

'You know, we've got to have food and at the end of the day we're helping to feed America.' Barb shrugged.

Like so many other factory farmers I'd met, Chip and Barb coddled themselves in a warped reassurance that they cared about their animals and that what they do is ultimately 'good'. But what I observed next just didn't fit with what your average person would consider good, or caring behaviour.

I'd noticed another bird slowly crawling across the floor towards a feeder. He was using his wings instead of his useless legs. With a little leverage from them, he had a chance of reaching some food.

I walked over and stopped close to him, so I could see how Barb and Chip would react to a bird in such dire straits.

Barb said, 'That chicken probably needs to be eliminated.'

Chip reached down and grabbed the top of the bird's neck.

'I just do it like this,' he said.

He then placed his other hand at the base of the chicken's throat, before jerking his hands violently in opposing directions. Then, holding the flapping bird in one hand, he started to swing him around by the head in large circles like a cowboy would swing a lasso.

This was just a game to Chip. He let go and the bird was catapulted halfway up the shed, landing in the dirt where he continued to flap his wings violently on the floor for several long seconds, before finally expiring.

Looking pleased with himself, Chip turned to me and then mimed how the company supervisors expected him to cull a chicken with a smooth and swift motion. It was vastly different from what I'd just seen him do.

'They don't want you beating on them and stuff. They want you to humanely cull them if you got to and you have to sign a paper once a year to say you know how to do that. It's not very hard.'

I was shocked at Chip's candour.

In my experience, the 'rules' aren't worth much in animal agriculture without supervisors there to monitor that they are being upheld. It seems that, away from the public eye, you could get away with murder. It was clear to me that Chip did, every day.

Shortly after that moment, I wrapped things up with Barb and Chip. I thanked them for their time and said that I'd be in touch if I had more questions about the property. Chip went off to get his fishing rods and Barb said she planned to make a cake. We parted on business-like terms.

Driving back down their gravel track to the main road, I noticed one of the wild children staring me down, so I wound down the window and nodded a goodbye. He responded with a snarl.

***

I headed to the city on a search for these 'special ones' Barb had boasted to me about. I was curious to see what they looked like packaged up on the shelves of America's biggest supermarkets. Joined by Leah – a friend and prominent campaigner for farm animals – we set about skulking around the meat-counters to see what we could learn.

The labels on the chicken in aisle fifteen of the supermarket that we were scoping out used some cosy words to describe the grotesque, bulging breasts on display. Words like 'tenderness', 'humane' and 'natural' were all part of the promotion.

We called the meat manager over to the counter to see what he knew about the rearing process. Dark-haired and bushy-bearded, Walt could have been a Nashville folk singer, and he wasn't shy about telling us what was so special about these chickens.

Grabbing the packet of chicken breasts, Walt quickly exclaimed, 'You see here, this is organic, which means the chickens are corn-fed.'

It wasn't an organic product. It didn't even claim to be organic on the label. Leah shot me a sideways glance as if to say, 'This is going to be interesting.'

'And this here says they're cage-free, Ma'am,' Walt said, thrusting the packet back into Leah's hands.

Then taking a few steps back to give himself more space, he spread his arms out wide and began flapping them.

'They were just raised running wild.'

For a moment it seemed as though he might take a bow as if standing in front of an appreciative audience. But Walt had only just got started. For his next act, he clawed back the packet and scanned the selling points again before settling on what the birds ate. Wide-eyed, we prepared ourselves.

'And it's what they call a *vegetarian* chicken… which I ain't ever had it, 'cos I don't eat vegetarian nothin' – I'm a meat eater you see.'

As he spoke, Walt folded his arms over his chest, very nearly making the sign of the cross as if to protect himself from the threat of vegetarianism.

'If y'all were health nuts… or tryin' to be…' Walt paused. 'Or care about animals, then you buy this right here.'

He tapped the chicken reassuringly.

Walt took a moment to look again at the packaging, then stepped back once more to give himself a little more space. He puffed up his chest.

'If you ask me, these chickens are spoiled chickens.'

By now his hands were moving in circles, strangely reminiscent of Chip's very own chicken-culling method.

'They can do whatever they wanna do!'

Walt was looking a little wild-eyed and breaking a sweat, and fearing a little for his health we began to bring proceedings to an end.

'That's very informative, thank you,' Leah said.

Walt moved back in close to us again and raised his right hand to the air as if testifying before the court.

'Hey, I'm just being honest with you, 'cos you know…' he trailed off.

'Do you know where this chicken's from?' we asked in unison.

'To be honest that I don't know, 'cos we get it from all over the country.'

With that, the performance was over. We thanked Walt and he shuffled off through the double doors of his cold section.

Walt had been shamelessly enthusiastic about this chicken as well as wildly inaccurate. Product labels and the imagery they conjure up in people's minds are incredibly powerful. What they don't say is certainly as significant as what they do.

Walt took his cue from the strength of a few words he'd scanned on the packaging and was able to create his own fantasy farm. But everyone wants to feel good about the food they eat, and it's people's willingness to assume the best when it comes to animal agriculture that keeps industries like this alive.

***

In total, I went undercover on eighteen chicken factory farms across the southern states of the USA over the course of a year. There were a lot of Chip and Barbs and their behaviour towards the birds was mostly comparable. Months after I completed my investigation, I asked a vet about the mortality figures on the data sheets that Chip gave me and they pointed out that the flock data from Chip and Barb's farm usually showed more mortalities than culls. In the vet's view, this was evidence of poor bird welfare management. In carefully managed systems, culls would be higher than mortalities as birds showing signs of poor health would be picked out during the daily walk-throughs and humanely euthanised before they could suffer to the point of death.

These factory farmers had become conditioned to be unsympathetic towards the individual needs of the chickens because they just couldn't see the individual in a shed of 25,000 identical-looking white chickens. Just as the industry had designed a fast-growing chicken that can barely carry its own weight, and removed it from its natural environment, they have also mass-produced a breed of unquestioning, uncompassionate growers who help them turn a chick into a profit in just seven weeks.

These are people who just aren't interested enough in chickens in the first place to ever be considered guardians of their welfare. After all, they don't even own the chickens. They're just keeping an eye on them for someone else and, when no one's looking, they can, and do, get away with anything they want.

Real-Life Davy Crockett

Despite everything that I had seen in my years as an under-cover activist, nothing could have prepared me for this moment.

In the middle of the freezing river, half-submerged beneath the water line, a raccoon sat hunched. I knew what was keeping him there, as I had accompanied fur trapper Mitch the day before, and watched him conceal a trap under the water.

I've seen and documented first-hand so much animal suffering that I have a huge memory bank of tragedies that just won't fade away. From time to time, something will happen in the present which triggers a recall of a particular moment and then I'll be forced to relive it. But this raccoon was different. I think about him every day, for his death was one of the most upsetting things I've ever seen.

It was 2010 and I was in the USA, deep undercover on an infiltration project for a coalition of NPOs, who wanted me to document fur trapping. A public exposé of this industry had never been achieved before so this project was of high value to the anti-fur movement, but it was also high-risk.

While most fur is farmed these days, around 15 to 20 per cent of global fur production is still sourced from the trapping of wild animals.[1] Few things stay the same over the course of 500 years, but fur trapping hasn't strayed too far from its roots. That's apart from the fact that most people now wear fur for high fashion rather than for the basic necessity of staying warm. Just as it was in the sixteenth century, when Native Americans first began trading their animal furs with French explorers, North America is still the key producer. In the USA alone, between 3 and 5 million wild animals are trapped for their pelts each year.[2]

1. http://britishfur.co.uk/the-fur-trade/production/
2. https://awionline.org/content/trapping-and-penning

And, while trapping equipment has evolved a little, the actual act of trapping a wild animal hasn't. Figuring out a good location, setting the trap and applying a scent to make it attractive to a particular species is knowledge that gets passed down from father to son or trapper to trapper and, because of that, the method has stayed pretty much the same.

So, over the course of two winters, I learned to become a fur trapper – a bad one, a trapper who showed enthusiasm and a passion to get out into the great outdoors but who couldn't catch anything himself. To the trappers, I was useless, an oddity and a bit of a laughing stock but, while I couldn't capture animals, I could capture the activity of the trappers. I was good at that.

I'd prepared for this assignment in the same way that I do each time when I go into the field. I serviced my camera kit, sourced extra batteries and bought external hard drives, which I can copy and where I can safely store hours of footage. I'd also done my research on the industry, joined trapping forums, subscribed to relevant journals and publications, and created my cover story. I had made myself as ready as I could be.

There are a number of different types of trap used to capture wild animals in North America. Their favourite, though, is the leg-hold trap. This trap – also known as a foot-hold trap – has hefty springs, a metal foot plate and powerful steel jaws, which slam shut onto an animal's leg once triggered. As leg-hold traps can easily break a leg, they have been banned in the UK since 1958, then a little later across the whole of Europe and across the world in eighty-eight countries.[3] However, they remain the go-to trap for many fur trappers this side of the Atlantic.

I used the fact that they had been banned in many countries as the foundation for my cover story. I started hanging out at the trapping

3. https://www.caft.org.uk/trapping.html and https://www.fishwildlife.org/application/files/9515/2106/4843/2016_Summary_of_Trapping_Report_Final_Draft.pdf

supply stores, waiting for trappers to arrive with both pelts and a shopping list of what they needed to keep their trapping lines active. While I waited, I would make small talk with the owners. I'd tell them how I'd always had a fascination for the world of the fur trapper. First as a child, when I read books about legendary frontiersmen such as Daniel Boone, Davy Crockett or Jedediah Smith; and now in later life, when I wanted to experience it for myself. Given that fur trapping was now frowned upon in Europe, I told them I had to travel here, to the birthplace of fur trapping, if my dream to trap were to become a reality.

The owners liked what they were hearing and, because their clientele were regulars, offered to hook me up. When trappers came in, they'd be asked to take 'the Brit' out on a trapping excursion. This was definitely a good tactic and one I repeated across a few supply stores in different states and provinces to help build and then maintain these unusual relationships.

But my first 'placement' didn't start out well. The first group of trappers I met were part-timers who worked the night shift at a prison. They then trapped together in daylight hours. Hunting as a pack, they rode quad bikes through deep snow in camo clothing most days so they could check a long line of traps they had buried across field and forest.

They were loud and they were mean. I felt sorry for the prison inmates under their care, let alone the animals they hunted. In fact, I wouldn't want them as my worst enemy. They were a tight-knit group; constantly suspicious and maybe a bit too savvy as a starting point for me on this project. While they were supposedly on the right side of the law, I sensed they were dangerous, and early on I deemed the risk too high to stay on to document them.

Instead, I ended up with Brad and Joe, or 'America's Worst Trappers' as I remember them. It was through trapping with them that I learned how to make a hash of everything. These guys couldn't catch a cold, let alone a wild animal, so while in one sense they were perfect for me to learn how to make a trap look good but fail to operate, they weren't much good from an evidence-gathering perspective. Brad had recently been released from prison. He had shot a man and was still under some jurisdiction, which meant his firearms were locked away at the local police station. I was happy about that, but it was also a reminder that trappers can be violent to people, as well as animals, and that I should keep my wits about me. Joe wasn't particularly bright and followed Brad about like a little puppy, even though he hated little puppies or anything furry for that matter.

I'd meet them each morning in a Walmart car park. It was my suggestion so I could keep them off the scent of where I was staying: a dirty, flea-infested motel, which had more wildlife inside it than I saw in an entire week trapping with these two.

From Walmart, we'd head out to the various locations where the traps were set. Parking Brad's supersized truck on gravel tracks, we'd march in unison across boggy marshes to inspect beaver traps. Each time we returned to the traps, we would find them as we'd left them the day before – empty. Gnawed-down sticks littered the immediate area, a sure sign the beavers were close but not close enough to earn Brad and Joe $15 for a pelt. They could easily outsmart Brad and Joe. I admired everything about them (the beavers, not America's Worst). They built incredible lodges, created environmentally sensitive waterways and kept nature in check – in a good way.

The closest we got to a capture was a little bundle of squirrel fur that was hanging by a thread between the closed jaws of the leghold. A lucky escape for the squirrel. Brad and Joe weren't too bothered, as they'd get very little money for the time needed to skin such a small animal.

After a week of this, I moved on. I kept the contact with Brad and Joe open, just in case I needed to return but I headed back east a few hundred miles to a fur-trapping set-up that was far more professional.

***

I met Larry in Rita's trapping store. Rita was showing me how to get the pelt off the back of a fox. Her husband and business partner, Bill, waited for customers from behind a glass-fronted counter that contained lures – obnoxious smelling scents made from dead animals' glands. The caps were screwed down tight – they had to be – but it wouldn't be too long before I got to smell those products at first-hand.

Bill, or 'Big Bill' as Rita called him, sprawled out across the counter and he did little other than eat peanuts while watching Rita run around doing all the in-store jobs. Rita was super friendly and, when Larry walked in, she got to work on setting me up with my next trapper.

'Hey, Larry. How'd you fancy taking Rich here out trapping? He's from the UK and wants to be a real-life Davy Crockett!'

'Well, I guess that'll be OK, Rita.' Larry shrugged.

Larry was pretty low-key. He spoke softly and sounded a little bit like Elmer Fudd. But he was a professional. He was the real McCoy and, according to Rita, he was the best trapper for 200 miles.

He wore head-to-toe camouflage, which in a store with a lot of camo accessories made him blend in pretty well. At times I struggled to find him just a few feet away. He was in his late fifties. Strong and with a face full of dense stubble, he looked like a mountain man, and I'd been told that mountain men knew how to trap. I'd tried my best to blend in. I had a trucker's cap that I'd broken in by kicking it around in the dust and then spilling some coffee on it; I grew a handlebar moustache and was decked out in jeans and a camo jacket. My accent was always going to set me apart, though in a good way. It was unusual for someone like me to be somewhere like this, wanting to be someone like them, and that made me a novelty.

I followed Larry back to his house. Set back from a small provincial road, his plot followed the curves of the river. Larry's place was typical of the area – wooden boards clad the house and an American flag stood proudly in the wind breezing in off the river. To one side was a garage, where Larry got to work. Inside, the walls were covered with furs. It was easy to identify what animal they were from, stretched out as they were across wooden boards. Grey and black rings signified a raccoon, the glistening golden red hairs were from foxes, and there was also a bobcat, muskrat, coyote, mink, river otter and the very recognisable rubbery flat tail of a beaver. There was a lot of fur in here and it was clear this man knew what he was doing. Larry showed me boxes that were full with hundreds of traps. With an air of nonchalance, he explained what they were for and how to use them. Some were designed to be buried under the earth, while others could be set underwater. Then there were snares too – metal cables that could be looped across an animal track that, once triggered, could choke an animal. It was mind-boggling and a real throwback to how I imagined the first trappers' sheds might have looked like. And it reeked; the smell was so bad. After Larry had stripped back the flesh from the pelt (known as 'fleshing' to trappers), he would then concoct his own lures from the animal's organs and glands. He would place these scents once a trap had been buried in the ground to bring in a victim. He had a lot of victims and a business-like approach to his chosen profession.

We agreed to meet the next morning at 7 a.m.

I arrived dead on time and found Larry hitching up the quad bike on the back of his pickup truck. We would mostly be using this to check his trap line.

'How long's your trap line, Larry?'

'The longest it gets is one hundred and ten miles [177 km]. Then I'll have two hundred traps set out.'

We didn't check all that in one day; instead, we would usually spend five or six hours checking a section of it.

My first day was a real baptism of fire. I watched Larry deal with a red fox with unnecessary brutality. The young male had his front left paw firmly wedged in the leg-hold trap. While snow sat on the ground right across the field, a ring of dirt circled the fox, evidence that he had tried valiantly, but unsuccessfully, to break free of the callous device. Larry approached him slowly. He was concerned the fox had some mange (a skin disease caused by mites) and said he didn't want to get it on his clothes, of all things. This was a man who already smelled like death, given his preference for making his own lures.

Larry pulled out a long pole with a metal wire attached to its end, which he looped around the fox from a distance to help restrain him further. Then he walked over to the fox and stamped down firmly on its ribcage. I heard the bones break and the air squeeze out from his lungs. I turned away to retch but recovered enough to stop myself from being physically sick. Larry didn't see me. All his energy and focus was going down into his boot and onto the fox's chest.

When the fox was dead, Larry turned to me.

'Pretty thing,' he said as he tossed it onto the back of the quad bike.

I asked Larry about the method he chose to kill this fox.

'I thought you'd use a gun, Larry. Isn't it easier that way?'

'I want to keep the pelt in the best condition. Putting a bullet hole in it won't do that and I'll lose money from the sale, so that's why I use my boot. I'll get twenty dollars for this.'

I thought about all the red fox furs hanging up on the stretching boards back on Larry's garage wall. These would definitely add up and I could see how you could make a professional career out of trapping. But the red fox wasn't really where the real money was for Larry. He'd shown me some of the bobcat furs that he'd caught on a month-long trip out west in New Mexico. He would get more than $500 a piece for these when the fur brokers showed up to source furs for the international auctions.

With the fox secured firmly to the back of the quad bike, Larry told me to jump back on. There were at least forty more traps to check that day and he said it was too cold to stand still for long.

There was nothing more to be found in the traps until the last one of the day. Up until that point, the cold had frozen the mechanisms on most of the leg-holds, so Larry had to reset them. I was his lackey, passing everything he needed from the back of the quad and learning the process and order for how everything was set up.

The last trap had been triggered and, even from a distance, I could tell from the black-and-white stripes on show it was a skunk. I'd never seen one before in the wild but I knew that their reputation for having the most pungent anal glands was not undeserved.

Larry sent me in to check on it. I walked to within about a couple of yards and stopped.

'It's not moving, Larry, I think it's dead.'

I inched a little closer and then the skunk's feet began to stamp and I could hear her hissing. I wasn't aware this was part of a pre-spray behaviour and, besides, I figured I was still far enough away to avoid any spray.

Wrong. It turns out a couple of yards is well within spraying range for a terrified skunk and she let me have it (good for her). Larry let me have it too. First, a roar of laughter, then the sound of a gunshot rung out through the ice-cold air. Turning quickly away from the skunk, towards Larry, I realised he had fired a handgun at the animal.

'You could have hit me!'

'I knew what I was doing,' said Larry calmly.

I think he saw this as some kind of initiation for me. Not wanting to take it badly for fear of losing his interest, I chose to laugh it off. It turned out Larry had no intention of taking the skunk's fur, so a gunshot didn't matter on that occasion. He stomped through the snow, bent down and picked up her lifeless body. Without a moment's hesitation, he hurled her off into the bushes. So she suffered, and died, for nothing.

On the drive back to Larry's I thought about the poor fox and then the skunk, who could never have escaped that trap, even with the best defence mechanism in the world. Larry was laughing at how bad I smelled. I didn't need him to spell it out. He then told me something I didn't expect.

'You smell just like the animal rights protesters I spray each year at the National Trappers Conference.'

'Oh yeah,' I said hoping he would tell me more.

'Yep, I mix up a batch of foul-smelling odours – including skunk – and, as I drive through the entrance, past the banner-waving hippies, I just give the spray bottle a shake and push down on the nozzle.'

Larry had a little chuckle to himself.

Of course, I chuckled along with him but, as an activist, I knew he was the one being punked this time. With the sun right out front, I pulled the peak of my cap down to shield my eyes and set the seat recliner into motion. Leaning back, I could feel the warmth of the camera inside my jacket. I was relatively content knowing there was still juice in the battery and everything I'd seen that day had been captured and would ultimately go on the record.

Larry went off to have dinner with his wife and daughter and we arranged to meet again the next day at the same time. He also had some work to do for the local church, with which he was involved at a community level. I headed back towards the motel intending to copy up notes and review footage, but I was exhausted and needed a little time out just to be a 'normal' person for a few minutes. So first

I stopped at a roadside bar, pulled up a stool and ordered a beer. The beer arrived at the same time as the dissent.

'I smell skunk!' someone hollered out.

'God damn, who the hell!?'

There was nearly a riot and most people left the bar, including me. The smell had become unbearable. I hadn't even taken a sip of my beer. By this time, I knew I had to ditch the clothes. I tried washing them in the motel's washroom but they came out smelling just as bad as when they went in. So I threw them away and got myself some more camo. It wasn't difficult in these towns, it was everyone's first fashion choice round here.

The next morning Larry let me into a secret. As we prepared to get into the pickup truck, he got a camera out of his jacket and turned the dial to play mode. He passed it to me.

'Take a look at those, Rich!'

As we drove to a nearby gas station, I flicked through the sickening images. Mountain lions writhing in the dirt trying to break free of a leg-hold, a black bear sat on its haunches with one paw firmly encased in a frame of steel and Larry holding a lynx up high by the scruff of its neck. In its mouth was a can of beans. The lynx was the can opener.

'Coffee?' Larry asked.

'Please.' I was raging inside at what I'd just seen.

Larry strolled into the gas station. The camera was still in my hand.

I had one, maybe two minutes before Larry returned. I opened his camera, took out the SD card, and zipped it safely into my jacket pocket. I then started fumbling around trying to locate one of my spares so I could swap them over. Inside the gas station, I could see the cashier passing Larry the coffees. I found one of my cards but it was still in its little clear plastic box. I scrabbled at the box trying to open it but the cold had affected my fingers. Larry was now opening the door of the gas station and walking out, so I twisted my body to face away from him. Finally, the little box opened and I dropped my SD card into the slot of Larry's camera just as he opened the driver-side door.

'Thanks, Larry,' I said as he reached out to give me the coffee. 'Wow, those pictures of yours are quite something.'

I placed his camera safely in the glove compartment, where I could get it again later and return the original card once I'd copied the photos to my laptop.

'Yep, me and my buddy got quite a haul out West, but we'll do better when we head south next month to Mississippi. They're so overrun with critters down there that, not only do I cash in on the furs, I also get paid by the authorities to eradicate the wildlife. And they don't place any restrictions on you, they just want rid of stuff.'

I nodded my head, but couldn't bring myself to make a light-hearted remark. No wonder trapping is so entrenched here when it's often those responsible for protecting wildlife – the state wildlife departments – who are usually issuing the licences to fur trappers – some for as little as \$10.[4]

I was a little way off getting in on a big trip like this but, over the next weeks, I did get to stay out with Larry at some of his trapping camps in the forest. With nowhere to hide, I was forced to spend all my time with this man. I had to talk like him, appear to think like him and eat like him, which for a vegan confronted with the 100 per cent meat-only option wasn't the best experience of my life. I managed to smuggle some of it away from my mouth and into my deep jacket pockets, but mostly I had to go along with it to fit in. I wanted to make a success of this project and I was in a good position to document what has to happen for a fur coat to be made, so no stone could be left unturned.

I documented a lot with Larry. He saw no contradiction in going

4. https://www.fishwildlife.org/application/files/9515/2106/4843/2016_Summary_of_Trapping_Report_Final_Draft.pdf

from a church service to setting cable snares across fox runs, which would slowly strangle animals to death. I filmed him hide the body of a pet cat in the brush after they'd succumbed in one of his cable snares. Trapping isn't just cruel, it's indiscriminate. Even federally protected bald eagles – the country's national emblem and a representation of freedom – have been victims of leg-hold traps.[5]

As for Larry, he showed no remorse. He just wanted to move on to checking the next trap.

As Larry prepared to head south, I switched trappers. This project needed to show what trapping was typically like, so I needed more examples to ensure that the final results could stand alone, and not be dismissed as a case of 'just one bad apple' by the government officials who would be faced with campaign calls to ban fur trapping.

I said my goodbyes to Larry. As a parting gift, he gave me a couple of old leg-hold traps and some snare cable. I forced out a handshake, jumped in my car and headed south to the next state.

***

Chuck had been trapping for years. He was always out on his trapping line and had already chalked up 400 fox kills that season when we first met. The season was only two months old.

He was bent over a workbench with his back to me when I entered his workshop. Between Chuck and me, hanging from the roof rafters, was a dead raccoon. I coughed to get his attention and he turned to face me.

'Hello, Chuck. I've been told you're the best in the state. I wonder if I could ask you a couple of questions about becoming a trapper?'

'What do you want to know?' came the curt reply.

'Well, how do you start out?'

---

5. https://www.bbc.co.uk/news/world-us-canada-38902572

Peering out from above his spectacles, he looked me up and down.

'Do a course, buy a how-to-manual, team up with a trapper,' was his response.

'Well, I was hoping I might be able to tag along with you,' I said optimistically.

'Oh yeah?' Chuck said while he pulled a fox pelt over a stretcher board.

Chuck was not as warm as Larry had been towards me and, though he took time to listen and then answer my questions, I felt he was a little suspicious. So, it came as a surprise when he said I could join him the next day.

Riding out with Chuck, we checked his trap line – eighty traps – buried mostly in the earth across three farms, where he had the landowners' permission to trap.

Chuck had all the trapping essentials that Larry had shown me but he also had a big stick. Last night at his workshop, he had told me his favoured method for killing fox was 'brute force'. Chuck was true to his word. I watched him strike a red fox around the head several times with that stick.

I got out my stills camera to capture that moment. My covert camera was running but I wanted to test the water about filming openly with Chuck to see what kind of reaction it got.

'Put your camera away,' Chuck ordered immediately before I could get any footage. I did as he said. 'I don't want you filming this.'

When the camera was back in my pocket, Chuck pointed out the eye bulging from the fox's eye socket. I wasn't surprised given the series of blows she had received. Given that Chuck sometimes led trapping workshops, the fact that this kill hadn't been clean had the potential to be embarrassing for him.

'Does that happen often, Chuck?'

'Not much – usually once in every ten kills,' he said coolly.

That would be forty foxes on his current tally for the season.

Just as Larry had used the force of his foot to crush a ribcage, Chuck, with the aid of the stick, had channelled the power of his forearms and hands into striking down the fox. Both methods were intentionally used to ensure not a mark was left on the fur. But they'd left a mark on me.

Chuck was also trapping muskrat and mink, so, before we wrapped up for the day, he went to check on those traps that were placed close to the icy water of a steep-sided river. I followed Chuck down the slope tentatively but had to spring into action when he slipped and began falling into the river. I grabbed his arm and the trunk of an aspen tree to break our fall and, once balanced, we clambered back up together.

'Thanks,' said Chuck begrudgingly. 'The trap's empty, though.'

'Can we arrange another trip?' I asked.

Chuck declined, saying he preferred to be alone when he trapped. I had wondered if that might happen. He was quick to take action when I brought the camera out and, given he was a higher-profile trapper, it's possible he smelled a rat. Rats wouldn't last long around this man, so I figured it was in my interest not to push back against his response but, instead, to start afresh with another trapper.

As I sat down that night to review the footage from my day out with Chuck, I saw that my covert camera was showing an error. All the evidence had gone. Body-worn cameras were pretty reliable but not infallible. It looked like the camera had packed up around the time I'd reached down to stop Chuck from falling in the river.

With valuable footage lost, I needed to make up for it with more.

***

I met Mitch outside his trapping shed. I'd spotted an advert he'd placed looking for furs when I was flicking through a trapping supply magazine and thought he'd be worth speaking to. I decided to doorstep him rather than making a call. It's easier for someone to say 'No' down the end of a phone than when in person, so I often just turned up unannounced. His pickup truck was full of dead muskrats and mink, and bulk bags full of raccoon tails littered the yard. He invited me in to sit with him by a wood burner in his shed and started to recount stories of his trapping successes. He looked like a clone of both Larry and Chuck. He had the camo uniform, trademark trucker's cap and grizzly stubble (more confirmation that my disguise was on point). Mitch, Larry and Chuck were very much a species of their own and, with more than 250,000 fur trappers licensed to trap across the USA and Canada,[6] they were hardly facing extinction anytime soon.

Mitch had water traps out for 'coon' and mink and it wasn't long before he took me out to what he called his 'honey hole', so he could teach me how to set water traps.

He set the traps – a single 1.5 in (3.8 cm) long spring and a double long spring – in shallow water and then pushed crayfish bait into a little hollow of a tree in the riverbank. Raccoons love to explore hollow logs and investigate around the rocks at the riversides. Once the traps were set and anchored down securely, Mitch said he was happy so we left, stopping only for him to show me some 'coon' tracks in the snow. I sensed he was feeling lucky that day.

Twenty-four hours passed and we were back checking on the traps. I was joined by Doug, a friend of Mitch's. He was a professional wrestler but was thinking of getting into trapping in his retirement. It had snowed overnight and it was cold.

6. https://www.truthaboutfur.com/en/becoming-a-trapper

Thankfully, Doug was wrapped up and not prancing around in his leotard.

As we approached, I could see there was a large raccoon sat in the river. His soaking fur clung to his skin and he was shivering violently. Most water traps are designed to drown an animal but Mitch said that some raccoon don't die by drowning but from hypothermia if they're in the water for too long. This raccoon was fighting hard against the cold, and he wasn't dead yet.

Mitch waded into the water with the big stick he'd brought with him. He swung violently at the raccoon, and I heard the thud as it slammed into his frozen body. This was the first of many blows. Doug and I stood back as Mitch carried out a brutal six-minute assault on the defenceless creature. I was filming openly but experiencing severe camera shake because I was so upset. I'd never seen an animal fight so hard for his life. I put the camera down on the ground and let that act as a tripod so the brutal scene could be documented properly.

Mitch couldn't take him down. Even though one of the raccoon's rear legs was being painfully secured by the jaws of the trap, he managed to grab Mitch's stick with his front paws and wrestle with it to stop Mitch beating him. As he fought for his life, I saw that one of his paws was actually missing. He surely had been caught before in a trap, so must have chewed off his own paw to escape. It's not unheard of for animals, in a desperate panic to escape a trap, to resort to undertaking their own amputation of a limb.

I felt a tear begin to run down my face but I knew I couldn't look away. Even Doug, a man who fights for a living, was upset. He turned to me and whispered, 'Isn't this kinda cruel?'

I had no words to give to Doug and I didn't want him to see my face, which would surely put my cover story at risk, so I just nodded my head in support.

Mitch was splashing about in the river in a fit of fury. He turned up the level of violence another notch and managed to get the boot of his wader over the raccoon's head to force him down under the water. Several times the raccoon scrabbled free and escaped but he couldn't do it forever. He was exhausted. Mitch's boot finally pinned him down beneath the water for the last time and he slowly drowned.

Mitch had given me his stick as he climbed out the river and, for a split moment, I wanted nothing more than to put it to use on Mitch. He walked past me carrying the body of the raccoon.

'Wow, that was a real wrestling match,' said Doug.

'Yeah, he took some beating,' Mitch agreed, fighting for breath.

The raccoon had looked big in the water, but now he looked sad and small. It took all my willpower to remain undercover at that point but, luckily for Mitch, I did.

I spent the rest of the investigation either out trapping, writing reports or logging footage. I also spent time filming at fur auctions where bundles of fur were being bought up by brokers keen to have their warehouses full before the international sales began. I knew I had a powerful investigation package and felt sure it would create shock waves across the news outlets of North America when it was released. And it did. It ran as an exclusive news story broadcast on CNN,[7] and triggered on the country's newswires a long overdue national conversation about the ethics of fur trapping.

But, before I flew home, I returned to the river where Mitch had his water traps. I wanted to say sorry to that raccoon for not being able to help then, but I promised him I would do everything I could to end this cruel trade. When I arrived, I

---

7. https://www.huffpost.com/entry/barbaric-trapping-not-rea_b_849278

found Mitch had left me one last piece of evidence. The season for trapping mink had finished a week ago but Mitch's traps were still in place. In one of them, a dead mink lay floating in the shallows, her foot firmly wedged in one of the leg-holds. I turned tail, raced back to my car, and returned with a copy of that day's local newspaper. I put the newspaper alongside the floating mink, so the date could be clearly seen, and took a picture to prove just how routine law-breaking seemed to be across this trade in wild animal pelts.

There were never any individual prosecutions from this investigation – the focus was to seek a fur-trapping ban and help turn the public away from fur in its entirety. The biggest trend in fashion right now is going fur-free,[8] and many of the traditional stalwarts of fur wearing – Prada, Gucci and Versace – are now advocating against the use of fur in the fashion industry. Mitch, Chuck, Larry, Brad and Joe may still be trapping but, with news like that, it might not be for much longer.

To this day, that raccoon exists in my heart, but he also exists on someone's back. Somewhere out there, he has been reduced to a fur coat or a trim on a hood.

8. https://people.com/style/fur-free-luxury-fashion-brands/

Fifty Thousand Residents

Were you not aware of the residents?' the police chief said.

'Yes, there were fifty thousand of them,' my colleague responded.

I was in police custody but I could hear the interview being carried out in the room next door through an open window.

The police chief responded, 'Not the mink, the farm's owners.'

I laughed.

They laughed too.

Going fur-free may be on-trend right now but, in 2015, over 40 million mink and foxes were reared and killed for fur on some 5,000 farms hidden across Europe.[1] The fashion industry's earlier backlash against fur in the 1990s had been well and truly forgotten. With climate change featuring every day in the news, the fur industry chose a 'sustainability' message to make wearing fur the right choice if you loved the planet.[2] Sales showed people were buying into it but, if those people really loved the planet, perhaps they would also care about the animals, if given some real-life facts about fur production.

So, documenting production methods for use in a national exposé was the task for this assignment. As such, I found myself working in tandem with another investigator – let's call him 'Greg' – in one of Europe's northern countries.

The fur industry is powerful and by that time had accrued a lot of experience dealing with animal rights activists over the past twenty years. With that in mind, we had decided to take an investigative approach that wasn't built around a cover story. Instead, we were gathering footage of fur farms covertly. We would work mostly from the perimeter fence but, if there

1. https://www.fureurope.eu/about-us/value-chain/

2. https://theecologist.org/2012/apr/10/cruel-or-eco-friendly-fur-ultimate-sustainable-material

happened to be a break in the fence or an open gate, then we would explore inside, making sure not to cause harm or damage to anything. Trespass would be the worst-case scenario if we were challenged and, in light of the public interest around this issue, it could probably be overturned in a court of law.

There were close to twenty fur farms in this country. All were rearing the non-native American mink. Smaller than an otter, their fur is prized by furriers around the world. They are highly intelligent, semi-aquatic creatures who are happiest when ranging freely across coastal habitats or inland waterways searching for fish, rodents or amphibians to eat.

***

We had to walk across several fields to access the first farm. The light of a summer's evening was beautiful but darker clouds that would call in the dusk were looming large. Taking a line across the trees to give some cover, I was enjoying these moments in what had been a damp summer at home. Little butterflies danced up from the field edges and the heads of the maize were soaked in golden rays.

At that moment I was far away but, when the long rooflines of the fur farm appeared over the maize tops, I was jolted back to the task in hand. Moving stealthily up to the perimeter fence, I could hear the murmurings of a little feed tractor.

The sheds were open-sided, so we could see some of the activity going on inside the buildings from our vantage point at the fence. The tractor was narrow enough to drive through each shed between two rows of cages and would dump little dollops of gruel on top of the wire mesh of each cage. 'Pup, pup, pup' it went, like a little outboard motor pushing a small dinghy along.

There was a lot of activity, despite it being almost 9 p.m. Three sets of scampering dogs' legs were pursuing the tractor wheels with great gusto; workers were hollering across to each other about jobs that needed doing; and, through our binoculars, we could see that mink were jumping around their cages in repetitive circles.

Each cage held groups of jet-black or snow-white mink. Some stood tall, with their front paws gripping the cage mesh, looking across at us. While the farms were well hidden from the public, it was clear we could not stay hidden from the mink.

Others were anxiously pacing the cages. Four steps back, four steps forward, rear up, paw the cage, start the process again. Their repetitive behaviour was extreme and, unfortunately, all too common for animals kept in cage confinement. Deprived of everything that would naturally enrich their life, it's easy to see how abnormal behaviours become a routine coping mechanism. They had already entered a world of insanity. When it's the fur off their backs people want, this industry offers nothing more than the basics – food, water and the most cruel of shelters: a cage.

Dusk crept in a little closer so, with a failing light, we gave up filming for the day. We took only the softest steps to walk away from the farm until we reached a point where we could re-enter the maize field. Making full use of the tall stems to stay hidden, we started to cross the field, heading back to the car.

Then the roar came and the chaffing noise of metal cutting across the plant. A combine harvester was in the field but, given the height of the maize stems, we couldn't see where it was.

'I can't see where it is, Greg.'

I think it's up by the woodland,' he replied.

'Nah, it's much closer than that. It's between us and the road – I'm certain.'

Up and down it went and the roar got louder and louder.

We had to find a way to cross the field, if we were to get to the road.

Like the flick of a switch, darkness suddenly arrived and the harvester's lights came on, shooting out shafts of light across the maize. It felt very extra-terrestrial, as though an alien space-ship had just landed in a field and was chasing us down. The blinding beams hit me full in the face and I turned my head away. Had they seen us? We were converging – a real-life close encounter. The noise was getting louder; the shearing of the blades was throwing itself at my eardrums. I couldn't see Greg anymore. As I felt this giant slicing machine move closer and closer, all I could think of was an article I once read about a man snoozing in a maize field getting shredded in the blades of a combine harvester. It was time to start running. I turned my back and at that moment, mercifully, the engine died. I recon-nected with Greg, who was only about 20 yards away and had also avoided an accidental shredding. We crept unseen through the maize past the worker who was now outside his cab, spark-ing up a cigarette, and melted away into the darkness.

I spent the next day avoiding maize fields. Instead, I found myself in deep woodland, walking the perimeter fence of another mink farm hidden deep in the countryside. Walking cautiously around the farm edges, we paid particular attention to avoid setting off the motion sensors, which had been placed along the fence at intervals. Visitors were clearly not welcome here.

Moving slowly through the brushwood allowed us time to observe the wider environment. I noticed a number of inter-esting things. The first was that there were data cards for mink scattered around in the woodland. The little cards would nor-mally sit in a metal slot at the front of each mink cage. They contained information about each animal, including its date of birth and medical history, such as the vaccinations they'd been given. This data was normally a vital component in evaluating the potential of an animal for a fur farmer, so it was unusual to find them here mulching their way into the leaf litter. Then my foot brushed against something hard. The leaves had given way to something sturdier, which made me stop. I looked down, and dark hollows, where eyes had once been, stared back at me. The skull was perfectly formed. It was not the only one. Within a few square yards, I found more of them, some with complete skeletons. I didn't know if there was a connection between these skulls and the data cards but, given their shape, they were clearly mink.

Were these mink that had died in their cages and been dumped out here with their data cards to keep mortality statistics down? Or were mink carcasses buried here once their pelts had been removed to cut back on waste disposal costs? Though possible, both options seemed unlikely, given that their carcasses are also valuable and used in the production of biofuels, or rendered into oil for cosmetics. Looking for more clues, I pushed deeper into the woodland, where I found a series of burrows in the earth, just wide enough for a mink.

These lifeless skeletons were probably escapees. Unsure of how to forage for themselves, perhaps they stayed close to the farm so they could continue to feed on the daily gruel that their former cage mates were receiving. Listed as a dangerous wild animal, if the mink were discovered roaming wild in the countryside, the farm would be in a whole heap of trouble. Poisoning would probably be a convenient solution and could explain the carcasses gathered together between the burrows and the fence.

I looked through the low-hanging tree branches to the mink cages. As they were open at each end, it was easy to see them. I could envisage a mink wriggling free and then skipping out to the wire when the cage hatch might have been opened for maintenance or a health check. American mink were a common sight in the countryside of Europe, despite not being a native species. Historically, fur farmers blamed mink escapes on activists releasing them from cages, while the activists would put it on failing farms seeking false insurance claims by releasing their own mink. There's probably some truth in both of these claims; however, I've no doubt that some mink will have taken a chance for themselves if an opportunity presented itself.

Underneath the mesh of each cage, I identified large mounds of mink crap. Like a series of organised molehills, they ran the entire length of the site, marking the presence of every group of mink on the farm. There were thirteen sheds, some as long as 80 m (87 yd). I totted up the number of mounds per shed length and factored in the number of mink per cage and figured a farm that size could easily fit 15,000 animals at a time.

It took us thirty minutes to walk to the furthest corner of the farm. This area was harder to access, so less cared for, and a break in the fence offered us an opportunity inside. While there was no physical boundary here, we still needed to out-detect the movement sensors. These were set a few feet off the ground and could be jumped or wriggled under. I opted for the wriggle.

By now, it was quite late in the day and the mink had all received their ration of food. There was no CCTV or worker buildings at this end of the farm, so crossing the cropped grass to the nearest shed was easy. As I peered inside, a whiff of fishiness swam up my nostrils. Their feed is a mix of fish bycatch (marine species unintentionally caught by the fishing industry) and animal waste from other intensive farming systems. I looked at the mink in the cage and then looked at their food again. I imagined the variety of DNA in this meaty mush, made up of animals that had been accidentally captured in a net or had also lived a life of confinement, and here they were fuelling another industry, the fur trade, exploiting animals for fashion. Let's be clear, the production of a fur coat requires more than the life of a mink – also the taking of fish from the sea and the incarceration of farm animals in cages or vast sheds. These are the hidden victims of fur farming. I doubt they were factored into any claims that fur was socially acceptable if you loved the planet.

Inside, the profiled metal ridge of the roof was just a foot or so above my head and sloped down to the eaves where the cages were positioned. There were four, sometimes five mink in each cage. Jet-black in colour, they were a little difficult to film in what was already a dark space.

In every cage, there was at least one mink that was as interested in me as I was in them. They were brave and confident and held my gaze with a stare of their own. For their brothers and sisters, it was another story. As I moved slowly in front of their cage, they would bolt into a wooden nest box to stay hidden. Then, one by one, they would gradually emerge and join their cage mate in a stare-off with me. When they were all out, I moved the focus of my camera over the nest boxes. They were tatty and filthy. With no bedding material inside like straw, they offered absolutely nothing in the way of comfort. Other than me standing in that aisle, their environment was devoid of anything that could provide something of interest to help them cope mentally in this cramped space. With no stimulation, a life in the most barren of environments could only lead to the stereotypical behaviours I'd seen at the previous farm.

Sure enough, as I moved through the rows, I began to see further evidence of that behaviour. Round and round they would go, stopping for nothing. I zoomed in on one mink and let the camera run for a few minutes and the movement remained identical for every loop. She timed it to perfection – there was not a paw pad out of place.

'Woof, woof, woof!'

The bark of the dogs broke my hypnosis. My gaze swung away from the clockwork mink to the outside.

I was a few hundred yards back from the farmhouse but it seemed the guard dogs had been let out for their night shift. With regret, I turned my back on that mink and returned to the woodland. I walked briskly at first, then started to jog. The dogs had a scent and it wasn't the mink feed. I looked back and saw four sets of eyes locked on to me. I started sprinting, camera bags swinging all over the place. I could see Greg was already over the fence.

'Greg, get the dog treats out!' I shouted.

With no time for a wriggle, I leaped over the motion sensors this time. As I leaped one way, a hail of dog chews rained down from the other direction. I landed in a crumpled mess to hear the barking had stopped. Looking back, the four dogs were lying down, tongues out, contently slurping on treats. Aside from one incident with a Rottweiler on a Polish pig farm, I have found guard dogs to be all bark and no bite, so a few distracting treats can be all that's required to avert a more serious problem.

***

The following morning, I awoke not to an alarm clock but to the clockwork image of that mink going round and round that cage, over and over again. I walked to the car with the hollow feeling that comes from knowing that she would have to endure another four months like that before the farmer came for her pelt. I took a sip of coffee and punched another set of coordinates into the GPS for the farm we were planning to visit that day.

This fur farm was structurally very different from the standard design used the world over. Here, the cages had been hidden inside a giant brick building shaped like an aeroplane hangar. It stretched out for more than 200 yards in a straight line. On arrival, my first impression was that there was no way it was being used to house mink.

At the top of the road was a small residential house. There was a house number but no other signage, like a company name or an old farm planning application that you can sometimes find stapled to a nearby post. So there was absolutely nothing to give any clues about what this place really was. With flowery borders and a variety of familiar shrubs, the front garden was neat and tidy – cared for. It just looked like a residential house.

We didn't want to pause for too long out front, so we parked up a few hundred yards from the property and returned on foot to a narrow path we'd noticed. The path ran alongside the brick building and was lined by poplar trees that stood rigid in the breezeless sky. As we walked the path, a few groups of cyclists peddled past and flashed warm smiles at us. In between those moments, when we were alone, we took turns trying to access the farm, pushing through bundles of greenery, mostly brambles with thorns that pierced our skin. Each time we were met by a wall of brick, just a few feet away from our faces. Then, just when we were about to give up on our recce, we heard a high-pitched, piercing scream. It was the call of a mink, coming from inside the brick hangar. Time to investigate. Fortunately, the path petered out and we found a field that offered access into the back of the fur farm, so we entered.

At the back of the farm, a track ran all the way down to the rear of the house. Hiding behind some old farm machinery, we watched the back window of the house for a little while. Now and again a few figures would move across it. With only the mink to be heard in the hangar, it felt like a good time to take a look inside. We waited for the figures to move deeper into the house, away from the windows, and then dashed across the track to the nearest door leading into the hangar.

The door was unlocked and slightly ajar. Inside was a little room given over to machinery and spare parts. A box sat on a small trolley which, come winter, would be moved into the shed's aisles. Workers would grab and toss mink from the cages into it, for gassing. This very controversial and painful killing method is used so it doesn't damage the fur. Given its size, the box looked like it would hold about sixty or seventy mink at a time. I shuddered at the thought of the carbon dioxide being pumped into a box full of panicking mink as I passed by into the main hangar.

If it weren't for the cages, the brick hangar would have been an amazing space. I could imagine some trendy hipsters from the city frothing with excitement at the thought of creating an open-plan living space out of this place. From narrow windows built into the curves of the structure, light streamed in and shone on the glossy black fur of the mink. It drew me in towards them. This was a two-tier cage system, spread out over four rows. The rows extended right down towards the main house. It was a pretty sizeable factory farm.

The cages at this farm were slightly bigger than those we'd visited before, so there was a little more room for the five mink per cage to move around in. But with territories in the wild extending to 6 km (3.7 mi), coupled with both the strong instinctual drive and the opportunity to swim and climb trees, this was yet another barren and cruel system for rearing beautiful little creatures.

I wanted to capture how little the housing offered the mink, so I began filming from underneath the cages. Peering up, I could see little paws scuttling over the wire mesh. Their pink paw pads stood out against both the metal mesh flooring and the darkness of their fur. Watching the swift movement of the feet, I could easily imagine them being used to scale up the bark of a tree, swim across water or cover big distances on changeable ground. A tear came to my eye but there was no time for any more. I heard workers begin to enter the hangar at the section closest to the house. They were on the move, shouting and bawling at each other as they headed up towards us. Greg was already making his way back to the door, so I stuffed my camera back in my bag and joined him, still unseen.

Poking our heads tentatively around the door, we could see a small group of people on the track chatting. We would not be able to get out of the hangar until they moved. Inside the building, the workers were moving closer to the section we were in. With the adrenalin pumping, a few seconds felt like minutes, so I was relieved when the group broke up, with some returning to the house and the others staying put in a lower section of the hangar. We sprinted across the open area to the safety of the machinery, then the field behind and finally the path, where we made our way back to the car.

***

The passing of the next few days was much the same as before. New coordinates were entered into the GPS each morning and farms tucked away from prying eyes were visited and assessed for their potential to film in. By now we had damning footage from more than 50 per cent of the farms in that country. I knew it would make a good campaign package when publicly released.

Having exhausted our list of addresses, we decided to return to a farm we had surveyed a few days earlier. We were initially put off by the solid fencing, which obstructed the view of the farm, but decided it might be worth another look. I dropped

Greg by the roadside so he could walk through the tall maize to the back of the property. Since it was maize and I'd developed a fear of combine harvesters, I was happy for him to be the one to do this. I drove off and parked up in an inconspicuous place about a mile away. We were sharing walkie-talkies. They are much more robust for this type of investigation and not subject to the signal drop-outs a mobile phone can suffer from. I kept mine close to hand awaiting news from Greg.

'I'm going in – it seems quiet,' I heard him say.

'OK, but make it quick,' I urged over the crackly airwaves.

A few minutes passed, without any more news. I'd turned the music right down on the car stereo so I wouldn't miss even the slightest of crackles.

It was such a quiet afternoon. Little traffic passed through the rural lanes. The day was warm and lots of little bugs were zipping around the hedgerows. Nature was doing its thing, unless, of course, you were locked up inside a fur farm.

I was tired and dreaming of returning home when a crackle on the walkie-talkie broke those thoughts. Then came a long pause followed by a series of clicks and crackles that I couldn't decipher.

'Aaaargggh!' and 'Get off!' came next, then a series of expletives that suggested Greg was experiencing some pain.

'They've got a baseball bat and they're not shy of using it!' Greg hollered over the walkie-talkie.

'I'll call the police,' I radioed back.

'They already have,' he said. 'They're on their way. You better get over here.'

'OK, I'll be there as soon as I can but I need to do something first.'

I didn't want to turn up at the farm with a car full of video cameras, tripods and tapes of footage from all the farms we'd already been to. I wasn't prepared to risk losing what we had gained so far. Instead, I chose to drive in the opposite direction until I found a quiet place where I could hide everything of value to this project.

A track bordering a maize field came into view. Putting aside my new allergy to maize, I took the track and pulled the car over onto the verge. I wasted no time and hid all the camera equipment a few yards back amongst the long stems. My notebooks that contained all the details of the fur farm visits to date, together with the location addresses, I stashed under a piece of corrugated metal that had been left to rust on the field edge. When I was done, I took a few seconds to look up and down the track to check if anyone had seen me, then jumped in the car to return to the farm.

I arrived there to see Greg being shielded by one of the police officers from a very angry farmer. Two other farm workers stood behind him pointing the finger and playing convincing henchmen roles. Red-faced and with spit flying from his mouth, the farmer turned to face me. With his feet dancing in the dirt, he began to charge but another policeman intervened quickly and led me back to my car.

'We're taking you and your colleague to the station for questioning,' the officer said.

'That seems like a good idea based on how angry that guy is,' I replied.

Greg was put in the back of the police car, so the young officer drove me in my car. He asked a few questions along the way and I was happy to answer them, explaining we were journalists doing a story around the fur industry. I showed him my press card.

'Why is your t-shirt all ripped up?' he then asked.

I was wearing a t-shirt that I'd ripped earlier in the week on some barbed wire at a farm. There were multiple rips, well, gashes really, which ran from my right shoulder right down to my left hip.

'It's a fashion statement,' I replied. The officer chuckled.

At the station, we were told that we were under arrest. It wasn't clear what the charges were at this point but they were exploring the trespass angle. We were placed in separate rooms but the officer who brought me in walked over to the window of the detention room and opened it. I went to the window after he left and peered out. My colleague was in the adjoining room and that window was also open. While we had our story lined up in advance in case of a situation like this, it was very helpful to be able to hear the interview next door.

A few hours passed before the interview process began. A public prosecutor had to be brought in from a neighbouring town and, when he arrived, the interview commenced. I heard Greg describe how he entered the farm and the moment when the farmer confronted him forcefully in the shed; and how the two henchmen blocked each end of the shed and were happy to join in with a little physical interrogation. As we had already agreed, there would never be any retaliation from our side if we were challenged on a factory farm, so Greg had not offered any resistance when attacked. Only now would we need to do that.

The questioning of Greg lasted about forty-five minutes and took a number of legal turns around whether we had notified the owners that we were planning to enter their property, if we were aware of the presence of any residential buildings and if anything had been broken to gain entry to the facility (it hadn't).

I prepared myself to be interviewed but no one came for me. An hour passed, then another and then several more until one of the young officers came in to tell me we would be released soon. I felt a sense of relief but it was muted because 'soon' didn't come soon enough. It was a few more hours before I saw the officer again.

When he finally returned, he asked, 'Have you lost anything?'

'I don't think so,' I replied.

He left again.

A further thirty minutes passed before he returned.

Again, he asked, 'Are you sure you haven't lost anything?'

When he had left me previously, I'd mulled over what he could have meant and there was only one conclusion I could come to. I had been seen dumping the camera equipment. There are always eyes in the countryside. But it seemed that the police didn't want to charge me with withholding information.

'Yes, I think I have lost something,' I replied cautiously.

I didn't need to say what I'd lost as the police officer said, 'OK, let's go.'

He led me outside, where Greg was already waiting and gestured for us to follow him. Weirdly we were heading to the back of the station, not to the front where we entered. Outside, under a carport and resting on the bonnet of a police car, there was a set of cameras, camera bags and tripods – ours.

'I think this belongs to you,' one of the officers said placing the equipment in my hands.

'Yes, it does,' I replied.

'I'm glad we have been able to reunite it with its rightful owners,' he said and winked.

'It would have been a shame to lose something of such value,' I said winking back. 'Thank you.'

I wasn't clear who had tipped them off about the dumping of the kit and tapes in the field, whether they had viewed any of the footage or, given that we'd left through the back door, whether the young officers had even notified their colleagues of this find. That moment, though, wasn't the right time to try and find out. We didn't want to stay long enough for anyone to change their mind, so we said our goodbyes. The only things missing were my notebooks and the address lists so we returned to the piece of corrugated metal under which I'd stashed them. Fortunately, they were still there, lying undisturbed in the loamy soil.

Then we were gone. There was no point continuing with the project after this incident as every fur farm for miles around would be on high alert. We had more than enough evidence of how the country's fur farms were run, so it was an easy decision to go home. We boarded a rearranged flight and toasted the police officers for their compassion. I didn't expect to be treated so favourably by the law, so it was a very rewarding experience seeing how these officers behaved. I really sensed they were completely with us on this project and, without them, the investigation could have ended in a very different way.

A few days later an article from one of the national newspapers had reported on the incident. It seemed the owner of the fur farm was fuming at our release. I'm sure he would have preferred if we had been kept behind bars, like his mink.

Our undercover investigation helped kick-start a major new campaign in that country to ban fur farming. Subsequently, in 2018 a national ban was introduced, so as of 2023 there will be no fur farms.

Second-Grade Life

Sitting in the courtroom looking at the stern official, I felt nervous.

My hands were clammy and my stomach was grumbling because of all the coffee I had downed in an attempt to keep alert. Fortunately, it was not me facing prosecution, but the owners of a pig slaughterhouse in Poland. A few months earlier I had been inside one of their facilities with a colleague. I remember the place vividly. On that day, I witnessed a live pig dropped into a tank of boiling water. Believe me when I say that's not something you can ever forget.

She had already been stunned – the process of rendering an animal unconscious by shooting a steel bolt into her head – prior to having her throat cut. But like so many slaughterhouse operations, procedures can fail. This poor girl had regained consciousness just as she was dropped into the tank designed to rip off all the hairs from her skin before the next stage of the processing could begin.

I saw her head flail back and her eyes open just as the tank door slammed shut. Then the shrieks and, worst of all, her legs kicking at the metal sides. The owners looked nervously at each other and the vet that accompanied us looked down at the ground rather than take the company to task over the huge animal welfare failure that had just taken place. Slaughterhouses are usually loud places. First, the animals are incredibly vocal; they know more than we give them credit for. Then there are the workers. They shout constantly to make themselves heard over the grinding cogs of machinery, which turn 120 kg (265 lb) of live pig into convenient, family-sized portions. On that day though, everything seemed to stop – except her.

I was physically sick that night. Even though I held it together to move on to the next part of the processing, I could not take anything else in. My head was full of the sounds of trotters hitting metal. It was just unbearable and now I was reliving it all over again in the courtroom.

***

It was a pig that escaped from the slaughterhouse next to my school that made me stop eating meat. I was thirteen and my parents had been vegetarian for a couple of years. My sister had recently decided to follow suit. With my face squished up against the top-floor classroom window, I watched aghast as a pig zig-zagged across the playground pursued by two men desperately trying to keep up. The other children laughed and jeered; it was like an episode of *Tom and Jerry*; that is, until Tom caught Jerry. We watched as the workers, with their bloodied aprons, roughly handled the pig. She screamed and kicked out but they had her in a firm grip. They dragged her across the playground and back into the slaughterhouse. Once the commotion was over, the other kids seemed to settle back down to work but for me, suddenly, everything my parents and sister were doing made sense. The next day I became – as the headmaster put it – 'a vege-what?'

I think I would have gone vegetarian sooner rather than later anyway, but I've always felt I owed that pig for showing me the way. So I didn't have to think twice about the need to testify against the cruelty I had witnessed in the Polish slaughterhouse. In the courtroom, I was shaking with nerves but tried not to let it show. As an undercover investigator, I was, however, worried about retribution. The meat industry has often been reported as having associations with the criminal underworld,[1] and though I had seen no evidence of that, anything I did to put some part of that industry in the firing line made me feel, rightly or wrongly, that I could be a target. The court had

---

1. http://bit.ly/2rgC6I8, http://bit.ly/2LoQcOs, http://bit.ly/2Ysj7qs

agreed to grant me anonymity when I testified, so I didn't have to face the defendants, but I was still concerned when I arrived in the country.

The company was successfully prosecuted. I was pleased with the outcome except, of course, for the suffering the pig had to go through. The case also helped open up media interest in the wider issue of pig farming in the country – the very subject I was originally there to unravel.

***

Poland had become a magnet for global pig producers by the end of the 1990s. State-owned farms were being sold up and big producers from Denmark and the USA were moving in to take advantage of the government's interest in intensifying their agriculture from family farm to factory farm. It seemed Poland was intent on going 'the whole hog' in becoming one big pig farm, surrounded by vast lakes of slurry.

Traditional farmyard scenes were eroded as vast sheds became the new neighbours. For the people living nearby, their windows stayed closed, even on the warmest of days. If they opened them, fly infestations would take over. Communities became invisible, living life in much the same way as the pigs did next door – locked up in a small space, denied both fresh air and freedom.

These vast warehouses of pigs were known as CAFOs (Concentrated Animal Feeding Operations) by the European and American businessmen who funded them. The farms are 'vertically integrated', meaning the companies that own them control the entire process from feed production to pig rearing to slaughtering. In the USA, it's often described as 'from first squeal to final meal'.

Most of the new farms were very secure, some even had raised security platforms like prisons; however, I managed to creep into a few. Some of my visits lasted longer than others. In one unit, while maintaining a tracking shot down through the main corridor, I stopped when I heard a noise that definitely wasn't coming from one of the pigs. It was a growl. A quiet, rumbling one but, distinctively, a growl. From low down, I turned slowly. I clocked the pile of slippery drool lying on the concrete floor and then the beefy mass of black and tan. As if in front of a dentist, the Rottweiler did a good job of showing me what he had. Free of drool his incisors were sparkling clean but I had no doubt there would be more than just denim between his teeth if he got hold of my jeans.

So I jumped in a pen with a group of large sows. There was little space for me, but I managed to get my feet down between them. Like a first-time skater on an ice rink, I moved slowly and unsurely towards the exit. The sows, whose lives I knew were devoid of any stimulation, thrust their snouts against me and shoved one another to reach me. I climbed over and through each of the pigpens. The guard dog followed, with that deep growl, sensibly sticking to the corridor where it was a bit cleaner. It seemed I was now the subject of the tracking shot.

In the last pen, next to the door, the dog and I locked eyes. I suspected he didn't know the Polish for 'fetch', but I tried my luck. I picked up the driest bit of pig waste I could find and hurled it back down the corridor. He bounded after it and I bounded out the door.

At the next farm, I met Christian. He was sat behind an imposing desk. He didn't ask me anything about my cover story – I was posing as a researcher in the agricultural industry – preferring instead to get straight down to talking about the success of his company's operation.

As was often the case in factory farm managers' offices, there was never much on their desks, and what was there was coated with dust. Everything of value to them – the pigs – was in vast sheds under lock and key.

A large picture on the wall behind his head showed a whale breaching the surface of a blue ocean. It seemed incongruous to me. I'd just returned from a trip around their CAFO, and was feeling pretty low. Tens of thousands of pigs were confined in darkness, unable to put their snouts through the earth to root out plants and grubs or to cool off from hot weather in a muddy puddle outside.

Christian lent back in his chair and put his hands around the back of his head as we spoke about pig performance data. It struck me that he was happy and free, like the whale, but only if every other creature near to him was locked up.

Foreign pig companies were only able to fund their massive takeover of the Polish countryside because of loans – some interest-free – from private investment funds or international banks. These are usually multilateral development banks, owned by a number of countries, set up with the aim of supporting economic development. Factory farming is also seen as development, though the loans are processed under the more finance-friendly term 'agribusiness'. Many of these bank loans are supported by the EU taxpayer's money. I was contributing unwillingly to the development of factory farming in Poland and across the world.[2]

Ever since my first project in Poland, witnessing the abject suffering that pigs endure at the hands of factory farmers, I've felt a special connection with these creatures. So, despite the horrors I'd seen, I didn't have to think too long or hard about taking on another investigative assignment into this industry.

***

2. http://bit.ly/2r8IoK7, http://bit.ly/2sJMY1C, http://bit.ly/2r8IoK7, http://bit.ly/2sJMY1C

Italy is a country that is especially famous for its food and, perhaps, the imagery that goes with it. Traditional practices of food production are revered and respected, get passed down through the generations and are marketed as artisanal, wrapped up in a Tuscan sunset for all to enjoy.

But, when it comes to meat and dairy, there is no romance in the reality. In fact, it's reported that almost all the fancy, prestigious Italian hams originate from factory farms.[3] This includes well-known products which have managed to gain Protected Designation of Origin (PDO) status, a sought-after EU trademark giving significant clout in the marketplace, despite being factory-farmed. Of course, the industry dismissed this as 'a blanket allegation' to attack their reputation and said that 'no producer had ever been denounced for animal welfare breaches.' There is nothing traditional about factory farming but, somehow, the artisanal tag has managed to drape itself all over this product, giving Italian ham a cultural status far beyond its borders.

I began looking for pig farms by following the curves of Italy's mighty River Po as it tracked across the agricultural heartland of the north on its way to the Adriatic Sea. There were a lot of farms on the banks of the Po. The river basin was fertile and a perfect place to grab water for both crops and livestock. Having travelled around the country previously, seeing the best of what Italy had to offer, I found the landscape here drab and uninspiring. It was made up of swampy meadows and vast monocrops. Few animals were to be seen on the land and utilitarian gravel roads led to the pig farms. Not the type of countryside you'd want to use on the labelling of your ham; you'd be better off leaving it to a marketing team to conjure up that imagery.

3. http://bit.ly/2Yn79hv

Admittedly, winter had set in and didn't help. The mix of snow showers and fog made it difficult for me to pick out the outlines of factory farms. But for pig investigations, you don't need to be led by your sight. It's the smell that tells you where to go.

I'd brought overalls with me but, once you've been on a pig factory farm, there's a good chance you'll want to bin not just the overalls but also the clothes you were wearing underneath them. It's not really the pigs. After all pigs, given the chance, are very hygienic animals. Though pigs can't sweat, they'll use mud to cool themselves down, given the chance. They'll also make informed decisions not to excrete near living or eating areas. The smell comes from something else – a mix of waste, feed, medicine and poor ventilation which, when combined, creates a substance that clings to fabric and tells every hotel owner you've just spent the day on a pig farm. I usually pack light, but I quickly learned that you need all the spare clothes you can get for a pig investigation.

***

I didn't expect to meet a Sikh on a pig factory farm in Northern Italy but, as I would discover, the Italian prosciutto business was very dependent on the hard work of those from the Punjab. In fact, Italy has the second biggest Sikh population in Europe after the UK,[4] and many of them are working on livestock farms. I'd heard it was because young Italians don't want to do this type of work anymore. Mandeep, who wore an immaculate, resplendent turban but heavily stained overalls, was open to me looking inside this farm. It was part of a business sending tens of thousands of heavyweight pigs each year into the prestigious ham pipeline.

4. https://en.wikipedia.org/wiki/Sikhism_in_Italy

Sliding back the door of the first big warehouse, I was faced with vast numbers of overfed pigs wrestling to get their faces into their feed troughs to nosh down on a second helping of maize, soy, barley and bran. The pigs here were all being fattened with the aim of reaching 180 kg (397 lb) as quickly as possible. To help the process along, the pigs were confined in tiny barren pens. The smaller the space, the less opportunity to exercise and lose the weight they were there to gain.

After they'd eaten, the coughing began. First one pig hacked away in a dark corner. Then two more started in the adjacent pen. Like a Mexican wave, the cough fanned out along the length of the pens and then returned up through the pens on the other side of the corridor. I didn't even have to ask the question; Mandeep could see it written across my face. He shrugged as he said, 'pneumonia'.

Mandeep asked me to follow him outside and then into a storeroom that doubled up as a pig pharmacy. I'd never seen so many empty medication bottles in a waste bin before – and one of my first jobs was in a hospital! There were numerous different medications but amoxicillin was the antibiotic of choice in this particular case. Even with the amoxicillin, Mandeep was struggling to keep on top of the infection.

He opened a freezer door and we stepped inside. It was littered with the bodies of the pigs that hadn't been treated quickly enough. Stiff and bloated, they had lost their shape and were beginning not to look like pigs anymore. But not every pig in the freezer had died from pneumonia.

Mandeep pointed at the scars that ran from head to toe across one body and slowly shook his head. These were scratches and bite marks sustained in fights with others. When stocking densities are high, and they were very high here, pigs will and do fight. A lack of space and abundance of boredom guarantee this type of behaviour. As long as pigs are kept in such conditions, there will always be victims like this pig.

The freezer was the size of a shipping container and, Mandeep explained, the piled-up bodies would stay there until the disposal truck arrived. It passed by every two weeks, usually about the time when the container was completely full.

'Would you like to see some more of the farm?' Mandeep suggested. 'It's rare we have visitors and it's nice to speak English for a change.'

'Sure,' I replied.

It was nice not to have to pressure Mandeep to show me more. He seemed happy to have my company. Usually, once inside factory farms, I'll need to keep gently coaxing workers to show me everything, especially when the novelty of my sudden appearance wears off – or wears thin.

Inside the next shed, the corridor was obstructed by a pig that had been spray-painted down the length of his back with a deep, pink line. Pigs that are sick or suffering injuries will often be marked out like this. However, given the dark conditions and high stocking densities, many symptoms or injuries don't get picked up until it's too late.

'He doesn't walk,' Mandeep explained.

Sitting unmoving on his haunches he stared blankly into the empty corridor.

Mandeep planned to leave him here over the weekend until a truck from Verona came to collect him and the ten other sick or injured pigs that had been left, unloved, in damp corridors all over the site. He was hunched over, clearly in pain, and had no way of accessing food or water without help. Seeing these animals abandoned, but still trapped, made me so angry. When the truck eventually came, it would take him to a slaughterhouse where he'd be processed for second-grade meat – probably pet food.

Some years earlier, I had been involved in a campaign to get farm animals recognised as sentient beings that have the ability to perceive and feel pleasure and pain. As part of a supportive animal behaviour study, a piglet and puppy of the same age were raised together and, during that period, undertook a series of tests to measure how smart they were. The piglet was by far the smarter of the two, learning everything and carrying out each task much faster than the puppy. The study helped get the British government to support the recognition of animal sentience in European law, but it took a European petition and a march by Europe's leading animal protection groups in Amsterdam before the EU's prime ministers made it legally binding as part of the Lisbon Treaty in 2009. Article 13 of the treaty states:

> In formulating and implementing the Union's agriculture, fisheries, transport, internal market, research and technological development and space policies, the Union and the Member States shall, since animals are sentient beings, pay full regard to the welfare requirements of animals, while respecting the legislative or administrative provisions and customs of the EU countries relating in particular to religious rites, cultural traditions and regional heritage.[5]

This statement has been used both with, and without, success as leverage by countless campaigners as they fight for the better

---

5. https://www.ciwf.org.uk/news/2009/12/the-lisbon-treaty-recognising-animal-sentience

treatment of animals. This Lisbon Treaty doesn't differentiate between species but, despite that, this pig was about to become food for a dog. His second-grade life ended as second-grade meat. We often hear people say, 'It's a dog's life,' when they mean that life is difficult and unpleasant. Try having a pig's life.

To help me gather more footage and evidence, I began working with Silvia, a very talented and committed animal activist who acted as a fixer, technical translator and chief distractor. Working with her, someone I could trust, opened up even more opportunities to take a look inside this secretive industry.

Maintaining the same 'agricultural researcher' cover story that had proved successful across all my assignments into the pig industry, we developed a strategy that allowed us to successfully document inside multiple farms. While she quizzed owners and workers, essentially keeping them busy, I got time to explore some of the off-limits areas – those places factory farmers are least likely to show you.

In one poorly lit shed, I jumped when I saw row after row of red eyes staring up at me from the steaming pens. The humidity was very high and condensation coated my camera lens no matter how much I tried to wipe it away. Filming was nearly impossible, but this was something I couldn't afford to miss, so I rubbed and rubbed at the lens to warm it up just long enough to keep the condensation off for a few precious seconds.

The bacterial condition the pigs were suffering from was a nasty case of conjunctivitis. Untreated, it can lead to blindness and there were several pigs that had reached that point – they didn't even register my hand moving across their faces. The conjunctivitis was so far gone that it was clear these pigs were not benefiting from any treatment, let alone the living conditions that would prevent this type of infection getting started in the first place. The pens were filthy and the pigs had very little space to move about. Like all the farms, there was zero bedding, just a concrete floor where waste built up. Pigs normally create a separate area to defecate, but in here they just couldn't do that. Every inch of floor area was given over to support the growth of the 'meat' and not the needs of the pig.

Every pig on that farm was without a tail. The curly, spring-like tail of the pig helps us define the animals' character, but in these prosciutto-producing farms a tail is an inconvenience. You see that when pigs are confined in such tiny living spaces and without any form of enrichment to help satisfy their curiosity, they become bored. Boredom soon turns to frustration and for a pig that often manifests into chewing the tails of their cage mates. Rather than give the pigs more space, enrichment or access to the outdoors, the fastest (and cheapest) solution is to cut off their tails. Mutilate the animal so it fits into the system.

Several days earlier, I had tripped over a bucketful of piglet tails. Like large worms, they laid lifeless on the floor, without a curl to be seen. Inside that farm, the mutilated piglets were growing fast into their metal cages but were extremely jittery when anyone entered the space. They bundled themselves into the corners, to put as much distance as they could between themselves and me. That didn't amount to much.

As I stared back at their tail-less little cheeks, I thought about all the joyful times when I'd seen pigs in nature. Even between these factory farm visits, we'd come across wild boar on forest roads. The youngsters sprinted around, hopping and jumping about. Life was just one long game. Their tails acted as a tightly coiled spring, propelling them forward into all kinds of fun and adventure. To me, a pig without a tail has been denied the spark that combusted it into life.

This routine, farm-wide tail-docking practice breached EU law. Despite that, though, from what I've observed, tail-docking pigs is the norm in this industry and most farms I visited across Europe were routinely snipping off the tails of pigs to help them fit into the barren conditions they'd built this industry on. It's a mutilation so culturally entrenched in intensive pig farming that many veterinarians must be turning a blind eye to it.[6]

***

It was a Saint's Day when I entered the next farm but, despite it being a public holiday, factory farms rarely shut down. This one was a breeding farm, a baby-making factory where sows had no choice about being a cog in that machine. Aside from short periods where they share a pen and can socialise with other females, a large proportion of a breeding sow's life – when they are either pregnant or weaning piglets – is spent individually behind the metal bars of very restrictive sow stalls, used during a sow's pregnancy, or farrowing crates. Both stalls and crates confine sows so tightly that they are unable to turn around, although farrowing crates provide space to one side for a sow to nurse her piglets. Usually, the sows are not provided with any bedding material. Pregnant sows have a strong instinctive drive to build a nest, but on cold concrete that's not possible. Stalls and crates deprive sows of almost all natural behaviours; they cannot explore, exercise, forage or socialise and these cruel systems have only been completely banned in Sweden, Norway and Switzerland. Most factory-farmed pigs will never go outside in their lives.

The factory farms that supply Italy's big ham companies make full use of stalls and crates to keep sows confined. I watched them sham-chewing and bar-biting, an indication of

6. https://www.eurogroupforanimals.org/disappointing-response-to-petition-calling-on-the-ec-to-end-pig-mutilations

severe frustration and stress. Welfare groups point to scientific studies, which suggest these stereotypical behaviours are akin to clinical depression. Feed, too, is sometimes restricted during a sow's pregnancy – as factory farmers seek to maintain the sow's bodyweight against the growth of her unborn piglets – thereby increasing the levels of frustration and creating periods of chronic hunger.[7]

As I walked the corridors for those few moments, I thought even the most die-hard meat-eater would struggle to stomach this system, if only they had the chance to witness it. I hoped the evidence I was documenting would give me that chance and, in this case, I was proved right, as our investigation was ultimately used to help start a campaign to protect pigs in Italy. It received more than 450,000 supporting signatures and the footage I shot was also featured across Italian TV news networks, including the national broadcaster, RAI TV.

In the next shed, a sow was having a fit in her stall. She was writhing on the floor when we found her. Collapsed, she was clearly in pain. We pointed her out to the farmer, but he said he couldn't give her anything to relieve the suffering. Couldn't or wouldn't? It transpired it was the latter.

'Won't you give her something to ease the suffering?'

'No, not today,' he replied gruffly. 'It's a Saint's Day and any intervention would be against God's will. I will do it tomorrow.'

I exchanged looks with my colleague. We were both shaken by his response, but clearly unable to convince him to act. He was one farmer keen to stay on the right side of God. It seems even religion has a say in how to run a factory farm.

***

7. https://www.ciwf.org.uk/media/5235121/Welfare-sheet-Pigs.pdf

It's only when you work on investigative assignments into factory farming that you become familiar with all the moving parts that go into the industry and how, if you only open your eyes to what's around you, everything becomes visible: the low-lying buildings, set back from the road, often without windows, the mounds of manure piled up like small mountains in the corner of a field, the feed mills towering over fir trees. The industry can be seen on the road too. Look a little closer at the heavy goods vehicles in the slow lane and you'll notice the livestock piled high in crates travelling up and down the autostrada, the milk trucks stopped in the lay-bys, and the feed trucks negotiating bends in the road to drop grain into pig farm feed-hoppers.

Round here they raced. Everyone did; even my fixer, despite my gentle attempts to get her to take it steady. It doesn't matter whether it's a Fiat Cinquecento or a 30,000 kg (30 tonne) truck, in Italy a vehicle is there to help you make up time. Unless you topple it, like the driver of the pig-feed truck who was in front of us.

I needed footage of the truck as part of a scene-setter for the film I was contributing footage for so, when we saw it pass us on the opposite lane of the country road, we found a place to turn and see if we could catch up with it. It turned out catching up would be easy. Just a few minutes down the road we found it on its side with feed half on the road and the rest trickling down a bank into a drainage channel.

'Are you OK?' we asked, winding down the window and pulling up alongside.

The driver was surveying the damage.

'Yes, yes, I'm OK, but this will get me into trouble. My boss won't be happy.'

We heard him swearing under his breath as we pulled away.

'That's a first,' my colleague said, and I nodded. If you search online for livestock truck crashes, you'll discover that trucks carrying live animals are involved in countless accidents on the world's highways, resulting in many innocent victims. Thankfully, on this occasion the driver was just carrying feed.

Pig feed in Europe consists of several ingredients but soybean meal is usually one of the main ones. A big chunk of it is now coming from the land grabs for soya that have been decimating the Argentinian forests. On a previous investigation in South America, I'd seen the devastation that soya land grabs caused at first-hand.

Forest communities were the big victims, seeing their houses torn down first and then the trees around them. With their homes gone and the land they needed on which to grow their own food now in the hands of thugs, they sat impotent under tarpaulins hung up between the only trees left standing.

And after the first soya is planted comes the aerial assault. Propeller planes swoop down to drop the powerful chemicals that are used on these crops to protect them from pests.[8] However, when I was there, it was becoming increasingly clear to me that the pesticides were probably having knock-on effects on people's health. So much so, that I was told by medical practitioners that regional hospitals were seeing big increases in birth defects, leukaemia and cancer rates in communities that were on the frontline of soya expansion[9] which many believed was due to the pesticides used.

But it wasn't just the peasant farmers who were affected. I talked to three mothers who said that, when the soya field first arrived at the edge of their town, they were pleased to have something attractive to look out on from their houses. But then

8. http://bit.ly/2YjFTAE
9. http://bit.ly/2ri3BkK

came the deaths and the deformities and now they could barely say the word 'soy' through their own tears.

Now, as I looked at the spilled feed trickling into another muddy drain of Italy's Po Valley, I was reminded of one particular peasant farmer I'd met in Argentina. Ramona was in her eighties and had been displaced twice before. Having lost another house to the bulldozers and having had her well and only water supply filled in, she was living under canvas when I found her. At her age, she had little energy to resist the land grabbers. During our discussion, I asked her about how she felt knowing that the bulk of Argentina's soya crop is exported as soybean meal so pigs could be fed in Europe's factory farms. There were no words, just a shake of her head.

***

My time was coming to an end in Italy, but I wanted to try accessing one more pig farm. Though it was a little late in the day, we walked through the gates of a large farm in the fading light for one last shot.

Upkar, another Sikh, met us as we rounded an office building. We spent a few moments talking with him and he told us to return later that night. He pointed at a crumbly house on the perimeter of the site and told us to knock on that door at 8 p.m.

This felt unusual. Often it takes time for a cover story to filter down to allow for a visit and then, when the doors do open up for you, it's usually during working hours. Still, with my flight home not until the morning, I had time to explore this lead.

At 8 p.m. I knocked three times on the door. The light was flickering from just one room inside. For a few moments, there was no noise. Then came the shuffle of tired feet, slowly making their way towards the door.

Upkar welcomed us in and then took us through to the room where the light shone. Inside were quite a few people. Predominantly family members and friends, almost all of whom were working on this pig farm or on pig and dairy farms in the local area.

Over tea, Upkar introduced us to several of his cousins. They were in their twenties.

'We have family in Birmingham,' they said in unison.

'Oh, that's nice,' I replied.

Upkar said, 'You are British, you will help them reach there?'

'Sorry… you want me to traffic them?'

'If I show you the pigs, yes, you do that.'

I'd heard something of the problems endured by immigrant workers, including the Sikh community, who suffered from poor worker rights on Italian farms further south.[10] I'd also read about workers being exploited and violently abused by gang masters,[11] so I shouldn't have been surprised to find some here wanting a new start. They were working long hours and received poor pay, so an opportunity for a new life could not be overlooked.

The project was risky enough, but this was one risk too far.

'Sorry, Upkar. I just can't do that, I'm afraid. I could get in a lot of trouble if I got caught, as could your cousins.' I could see they were disappointed. 'I should probably go.'

I thanked Upkar for the tea and saw myself out.

It isn't just the pigs that suffer in the production of famous Italian hams. It's the workers, the forests and the little old ladies who live under tarp far, far away.

10. http://bit.ly/33Rstgy
11. http://bit.ly/2ql52hI

The Belly of the Beast

The car pursued us at high speed across Bahrain's Manama City in the Persian Gulf.

Our fixer was rushing us to the airport through the back streets. In the car that was chasing us were the *real* owners of the 30,000 Australian sheep that had been offloaded in the city's port two days earlier.

The country had been out of sheep meat for weeks and even the government was desperately awaiting their arrival. When would the sheep arrive? That had been the question on everyone's lips, on the TV news bulletins and in sizeable column inches given over to the story in the newspapers.

My colleague and I had spent two days posing as the owners of the sheep. Adopting our Australian personas, everyone became our 'mate'. Well, up until the day we met the actual owners.

Prior to this trip, it had proven very difficult for anyone outside the farming industry to gain access to the livestock boats transporting Australian animals between countries, primarily because the Australian sheep trade liked to keep these journeys under wraps. Livestock vessels were off-limits to the public, as were the foreign slaughterhouses where the animals ended up. Australia is one of the biggest exporters of livestock in the world.[1] Their live export is a tightly controlled industry and is historically well supported by the establishment, even though public opposition to the trade is high.

Documenting a trade in the public interest but with little imagery to work with required a little bravado. It would take a serious bluff to gain access to Bahrain's slaughterhouses, feed-lots (areas of land given over to finishing livestock), ports and even a livestock vessel.

---

1. https://reut.rs/362ertG

However, over the course of a few days, we were able to do just that.

It started with a shirt and tie, then a smart haircut and some serious revision on sheep rearing and welfare. Finally, we needed a supportive local to help us move about the city and facilitate meetings and appointments. We lucked out on Khalid, who was the perfect 'fixer'. Fixers are local people who are employed to help solve problems. They're often used by film crews or international businesses and I would sometimes use one to help me find places or meet people in a country I didn't know very well. They're worth their weight in gold, can save you a lot of time and help 'open doors' with the local community. A local animal protection organisation had recommended him, so we knew he'd be supportive of our work. Khalid knew everyone – or at least it looked that way. He'd regularly stop the car to ask help from people on the streets or would be on the phone to port officials trying to get us an access permit. He was a great lover of animals too, which always helped with these projects. If we had a few minutes here and there between appointments, we would nip down to the local animal shelter, where we'd drop off some dog toys, and Khalid would have a quick game with some of the strays.

Summer in Bahrain was hot. Even the shamal wind, which funnels across the Persian Gulf from Saudi and Iraq couldn't take the edge off the heat. On that trip, it brought a choking dust from the desert into the city, creating its very own Instagram filter. The wind-driven dust and the searing heat were two reasons to stay inside if you could. The third was that the vessel hadn't yet arrived in dock, but we could watch its progress online.

Using satellite-tracking sites, we could follow the livestock vessel on its eighteen-day sea journey from Australia. It had picked up sheep first in Victoria and then in Western Australia before crossing the Indian Ocean and the Arabian Sea. During these kinds of crossing, the sheep – and cattle that are often also on these voyages – have to deal with rough seas, a lack of space, lying in their own waste, infections and often a range of injuries caused by an abrasive deck surface and poor drainage.[2] But it's the heat that really hurts.

The greatest threat for livestock on vessels entering the Gulf of Oman is not Somali pirates, it's the mass deaths of animals by heat stress. With soaring temperatures, the metal boats become ovens and, for the sheep – that means cooking from the inside out, with each of their organs shutting down one by one before death.

The Australian government accepts a mortality rate of up to 1 per cent on sheep exported by sea, and cattle and buffalo transported for more than ten days.[3] For those vessels capable of transporting 75,000 sheep, that means it's perfectly acceptable for up to 750 sheep to die on a boat in just a couple of weeks. Over the course of one year's worth of shipments, that figure can run into thousands of deaths.

Then there is what you would classify as 'shipping disasters' – and it's not just the Australian trade that's impacted. The global live export trade criss-crosses the planet, and it's left a mark on both the ocean charts and the seabed. Ships capsizing, mechanical failures, disease outbreaks and ravaging fires have led to mass deaths of livestock during transit.

The state of the trade and the suffering it causes makes even the most ardent meat-eater ask the question, 'Why transport live when you can send meat refrigerated?' In Bahrain, and in many other countries in the region, it's because there is a demand for 'fresh' meat. For several cultural and religious rea-

2. http://bit.ly/36h5UDF
3. http://bit.ly/33SfOK3

sons, the preference is for animals to arrive on the hoof, not the hook. Instead of losing out to another country, Australia puts ethics aside to keep the boats moving.

***

This boat sure was moving. Arriving at the port, I could see big plumes of black smoke billowing out from the vessel's funnel as it approached. It was as if it was in mourning. Even before I could see the boat, I could smell it. But it wasn't the smell of the smoke. It was a vessel drowning in urine and faeces, wafting in on a light onshore wind. There was no need for a news report or radio bulletin, everyone's nostrils knew it had arrived.

It had taken us twenty-four hours to gain access inside the port – even with our cover story that we were owners of the approaching sheep. We dished out cigarettes to the port security to help move the process on and then, eventually, a few emails were pinged out to someone we'd never meet in person, but which resulted in permission being granted. With a bit of persistence, it's surprising what you can achieve. The next step was more challenging, though.

The livestock trucks were already arriving dockside. They wanted to get the animals off straightaway. It felt like the public was already waiting, hands outstretched, ready to exchange money for lives. We waited for the unloading to begin, principally because the workers would be focused on that and we hoped they wouldn't pay too much attention to us. I had also noticed that custom officials had arrived to make some checks. The stars were aligning to keep eyes diverted from our activities.

When the gangway dropped, we moved, confidently heading across the quay and bounding up the steps of the boat's monstrous sides.

On deck, at the top of the gangway, there were two crew members.

'Hello. I own the sheep and want to check on the animals' condition,' I demanded in a thick Australian accent.

The Filipino workers looked at each other and then back at me.

'Please take me below now,' I said. This time I raised my voice a little more sharply.

The workers nodded but said they would get a senior official to OK it first. They looked nervous and worn out. Their clothes were filthy and it seemed like they had faced pretty bad conditions themselves. It didn't leave me with much hope for the state of the animals.

It's not uncommon to hear tales of the workers on livestock vessels – and indeed on other kinds of cargo ships – living in poor conditions. I once managed to make it onto a livestock vessel that was docked in the UK on its way to Ireland to pick up livestock bound for a war zone: Libya. The ship had been forcibly brought in by local authorities, following a mayday call-out during a storm in the English Channel. Once safely in port, the ship was impounded by the Maritime and Coastguard Agency on a number of safety issues, one of which was that the crew were said to be living in unsafe conditions.[4] That ship, too, was crewed in part by Filipinos. They were friendly and welcoming when we arrived – they'd been given a fair amount of support by the Cornish seafaring community that rallied around to help them. But, as soon as we asked to see where the animals were kept, everything changed. That wouldn't be possible. The best we would get was a look at the ship's blueprints (technical drawings of the vessel's layout) showing deck after deck of pens and the narrow walkways between them.

4. http://bit.ly/2PgYNnD

But we were in for better luck back in Bahrain. One of the crew returned saying the Chief Officer had approved our check on the animals.

The other crew member thrust a pen in my hand and passed me a clipboard. I scribbled 'A. Ram' onto the sign-in sheet and followed the workers below, down into the depths of the vessel. And it really was the depths. The vessel had already unloaded the top decks in Kuwait, the first drop-off point for sheep in the Gulf, and the remaining 30,000 sheep were right down in the vessel's hold – the belly of the beast.

It was dark and barbeque-hot down there. The stench was overpowering. The once-white merino sheep were panting in the thick air. With their fleeces stained faecal-brown, their bodies heaved up and down rapidly, trying desperately to regulate their temperature.

'How was Muscat?' I asked.

Muscat in Oman is the point in the Gulf where the sheep have to deal with extreme heat and high humidity.

'We lost three hundred,' he replied.

'Where do you put them?' I asked, hoping to see the bodies.

'The sharks have them,' he said as he grinned through his own set of jagged teeth.

I had asked the two crew a lot of questions, so many that they failed to notice my colleague had slipped away to document the sheep he hadn't shown us. A deliberate tactic we often employed, it gave us the chance to get the freedom to explore unescorted.

As we resurfaced from the dark, they suddenly noticed my colleague was gone and I was, of course, none the wiser to tell them where he was. With panic on their faces, they scrambled a few more crew together ready to undertake a search. But there was no need; with perfect timing, my colleague reappeared, with his camera safely tucked away in his jacket and a look on his face that said, 'I was only a few steps behind you this whole time.' I grabbed the clipboard that had been left out at the top of the gangway and signed out. As they tried to establish where my colleague had been, I waved my hands around busily at them and said we were in a rush and had no more time for talk and that they, too, should get back to work.

At the bottom of the gangway, sheep were being loaded onto the trucks but there were some who wouldn't be loaded. These lay dead on the ground – dragged out to make way for the living to pass.

Inside the ship, we'd both noted dead animals in pens, even though, as the crewman suggested, most of the dead had already been dumped in the sea or taken off at Kuwait. It was oppressive and filthy. While the journey would have been pleasant enough for the crew in their air-conditioned berths, travelling in the hold on tempestuous seas must have been horrendous for an animal normally found grazing on lush, green pastures.

As we stood on the dock watching the loading, a few of the workers casually asked us who we were. When we told them we were the owners, they sharpened up their behaviour. Their sticks and poles became less like weapons for taking out their frustration and boredom, and more like tools for carefully guiding the sheep onto the trucks.

The sheep did what they were told. They were lacklustre and still panting heavily, so not likely to put up much opposition to this process. It was immensely depressing to watch those poor animals. They had been on one hell of a trip on the high seas and now they would be driven straight to the slaughterhouse, where they would be killed immediately to offset the meat shortages. Normally, sheep would be sent to a feedlot for a period of time to recover and perhaps regain some weight, but not today. Even the walking wounded were taken directly to their deaths at the slaughterhouse, which was our next destination.

***

'G'day,' we said to the workers around the back of the building when we arrived.

This was a chance to get some secret footage so we watched the last batch of Australian cattle, from a previous shipment, slip and slide their way across a wet concrete floor to the knife that workers would use to cut their throat. Electric goads (handheld sticks charged with pain-inducing bursts of electricity) zapped at their hindquarters if they showed the slightest hesitation.

Inevitably, we were told to leave that area and go to the main reception. There we met the manager, Yousif.

Being sent to a manager is often a sign of the absence of the owner, which from our point of view was a good thing. It makes things less complicated. We trotted out the same cover story used to gain access to the boat but added to it a little, saying we were here on a fact-finding mission that could increase the number of Australian animals available to the market. Yousif believed this could lead to more animals for the slaughterhouse, so he was happy to talk. He also walked us back into the slaughter zone and then out into the lairage area, where they usually hold livestock until they are ready to kill them.

The sheep were 'processed' quickly but, like the cattle, were killed without pre-stunning, as a requirement of 'halal' ritual slaughter. Bundled through swiftly, I found the process, and the desperate kicks and gasps of dying sheep, hard to view and after a short while I had to leave.

I took a few moments to myself outside. The sun was searing hot, so I couldn't stand out there for long. I moved to the lairage area, where some of the sheep were now waiting as more trucks had arrived and unloaded from the port.

Thankfully, it was shaded and the sheep had some respite from both the climate and the people. But, of course, they were just a few moments away from the chaos. Nothing stands still for very long at slaughterhouses.

'Rich, it's time to go!' yelled my colleague as he walked quickly out of the kill-room to where we'd been dropped off by Khalid.

He had tried to get my attention but it was too late. Before I knew it, the Aussies had arrived – the genuine ones – and they had me surrounded.

Their smart branded polo tops and baseball caps showed they were the real deal. They were the official owners of the sheep and they had caught wind of some other 'sheep exporters' who were in town and trying to pull the wool over the eyes of this business.

'Who the hell are you?' was their opening question.

'Who the hell are you?' was my response.

By this time my colleague was by my side and, like a bad comedy double act, we volleyed their questions back at them as if it was they who were the dodgy sheep owners.

'Why are you here?'

'Why are you here?' we replied, dragging our vowels out to make us sound more Australian than they were.

It was childish, but it was buying us time.

'Look, we just want to know who you are!'

'Well, we don't have to tell you. You're not the cops, so we don't have to tell you anything we don't want to. Mind your own business,' I retorted.

At that point, I realised that's exactly what they were doing.

Just as it was clear there was no way we could keep up the act, Khalid intervened with a car door swinging out conveniently right in front of us. Before they could stop us, we jumped in and sped off, leaving a big cloud of orange dust circling around them.

But we weren't alone for long. We were being tailed by the Aussies.

'Khalid, you need to go a bit faster!'

'I'm going as fast as I can,' he said.

'Well, maybe you could put your cigarette out,' I suggested, hoping that would help him put both hands back on the steering wheel and speed up.

Khalid did as I asked, and the gap widened between our vehicles.

By the time Khalid had entered the back streets of the city, we'd shaken them off.

On the way to the airport, I felt a little bad wondering if the crew on the ship would face reprimands for falling for our story. A livestock truck passed by on the opposite carriageway and brought me to my senses. I reminded myself that, without these kinds of elaborate fabrications, it was almost impossible to really get on the inside of animal industries like this – and there was so much at stake. This type of documentation was a necessity; without it, we would know nothing of these poor animals' lives or deaths.

***

I'd come a long way since I can first remember a livestock truck passing me. On that day, I wasn't in a vehicle trailing but standing by a port entrance with a protester's placard. The port was Shoreham, on the UK's south coast, and the year was 1995.

At that time, vast numbers of sheep and cattle were being exported from the UK for slaughter or further fattening in Europe. Lambs could go as far as Italy and southern Greece, though many succumbed in the summer heat on those trucks.

Calves would end up in veal crates, a system that was banned in the UK in 1990 because of the suffering it caused.

This was a period when the British nation became not just aware of live exports but also concerned about the welfare and rights of farm animals in a big way. As a protest organiser, I spent many days criss-crossing the country's ports and airports, trying to prevent live animal exports. The national ferry companies had agreed to stop live export trucks using their ferries so the livestock industry began chartering their own boats and planes to keep the trade flowing.

The exporters jumped around the British countryside from port to airport, no matter how small. They wanted to get the animals out at any cost. However, they hadn't figured on Middle England joining the activists' protest lines and, one by one, their attempts got shut down.

Unlike factory farms, which hide farm animals from the public eye, this was a trade that became very visible for people of all ages and from all walks of life. Instead of trucks rumbling through the night – given cover by the darkness and the scale of a big transport hub – they were having to pass by communities, whose houses were built just inches back from the narrow roads leading to their town's little ports. Baby calves, bellowing for their mothers, could not just be heard but seen every time the sash windows rumbled with the passing of a livestock truck. That visibility became a catalyst for people power and soon the roads around these ports were blocked by the locals. Even the law seemed powerless to stop the protests, which had escalated to include the ports of Brightlingsea and Plymouth and the airports of Prestwick, Carlisle and Coventry. British ports and airports became focal points for protest and some police officers found themselves with the task of policing their own family members who were linking arms with their neighbours in the street outside their homes. It was always going to end badly for the live exporters and now the UK trade is down to just a trickle of a few tens of thousands from its mid-1990s highs of 2.5 million animals a year.[5]

Since those early protests, I have always been interested in doing as much as I could to open people's eyes to this global trade; after all, I'd seen it was an issue that had the potential to mobilise people into activism. Over the years, I've travelled to Singapore to document the airfreighting of Irish and Australian sheep for use in religious slaughter festivals and I've been stuck at the Russia–Belarus border for days in minus 20 degrees Celsius, tracking the route of pregnant heifers taken to breeding farms desperate for European livestock. I've also filmed after dark in Israeli ports and fattening farms. It's a country whose coastline is fast becoming a graveyard for European livestock: dumped overboard, cattle carcasses wash up with the first waves of the day to break on the beaches south of Tel-Aviv.

Sadly, animal suffering often begins at the origin of these journeys, particularly when animals are first loaded onto trucks. The trigger point comes when trying to cram a few more animals on board. As soon as a truck becomes overcrowded, the first injuries tend to show up. It could be a broken leg from a sheep getting stuck in the truck slats or an eye injury to a cow from another's horn. But sometimes livestock can be trampled to death. And when animals are in transit for several days or more, they can and do die from exhaustion or dehydration through extreme temperatures or lack of sufficient food, water and rest.

When following these animals, it's easy to sympathise with how they suffer during these journeys. I found trailing the trucks over vast distances and multiple countries in Europe

5. http://bit.ly/2DRkd5n

completely debilitating, even when sharing the driving with a colleague. It was very difficult to rest, as we had to react to everything the truck drivers did. They were in control. They, not us, knew where they were going, so we had to be prepared for anything. Mentally I was exhausted after each trail and sometimes, like the animals, I finished these assignments with physical injuries of my own. Two incidents left dents in my head but they never led me to question whether this was the right thing to be doing with my life.

***

On one occasion, the livestock driver we were following had been on the road for a couple of days, travelling down through Ireland and France towards his ultimate destination, Spain. Staying undetected in a following vehicle is the standard practice for trailing assignments. With a little knowledge and experience, it's quite possible to tail a truck for several thousand miles without getting noticed. The important thing is to stay back unless you're in urban areas when you need to stay very close, especially if there's a set of traffic lights, a junction or a roundabout with multiple exits. That's when you can lose a truck.

But staying incognito does get tougher the closer you get to the final destination of any trail and in Spain we were clocked by the driver as he pulled over into a lay-by on a very narrow country track. Rather than sit tight in the car when I realised that he had worked out he was getting tailed, I did what I always do in this situation: go and talk with the driver. It might be the last chance to check on the condition of the animals after a long journey in the summer heat.

He wasn't Glaswegian but it transpired he knew how to 'kiss' like one: the butt of his head thundered into my cheek just below the eye socket after I introduced myself.

'Ouch,' I said as I fell over.

'You had better stop following me as you'll get a good pasting next time.'

My head was thumping and, kneeling on the ground, I was grateful that was all I got. It would have been easy for him to send one of his boots into my teeth as well.

We followed initially but things got a little heavier for us after that, as he had promised.

'I think we've got company,' I said, still nursing the blood trickling down my face.

'Oh yeah, I see them,' my colleague replied while staring at the rear-view mirror.

Several cars were driving erratically behind us and then one pulled up alongside our moving car. The passenger smiled at me before raising a wooden club from his lap. He took to smacking it repeatedly into the palm of his free hand.

'Time to bail out,' I told my colleague and we took the next slip road out of there.

Even so, I had another crack at documenting this route. On a subsequent investigation, we kept well back, as much as we could without losing the livestock vehicle, and followed the young cattle all the way into the Spanish slaughterhouse. Without seeking permission, we tried our luck and walked around the building to a side entrance, which was only screened off by strips of plastic. So we went inside and began openly filming the slaughtering.

'Get out!' one of the workers shouted when he saw the camera. 'You must get permission from the office if you want to be in here!'

'OK, no problem,' we said in our broken Spanish.

Instead of going to the office, we waited outside the plastic screening alongside the wall. We allowed five minutes to pass before we returned to the slaughter area. The workers looked at us and we gave them the thumbs-up sign, which they took to mean that we had our permissions.

Luck like this is a rarity and, of course, it didn't last. As I made my way across the killing floor, I suddenly came crashing to the ground. With my eye firmly locked on the camera's viewfinder, I hadn't noticed that I had placed myself in between a slaughter worker handling a cow's remains and a waste bin. I didn't see the hoof come hurtling towards me and I don't even remember it slamming into the side of my head, knocking me unconscious for a short while. It wasn't intentional on the worker's part – I'd just found myself in the wrong place at the wrong time. When consciousness did return, I found myself lying in a thick pool of deep-red blood. Initially, I thought my injury was far worse than it was. How did I lose so much blood? Was this the end? As I regained clarity, and my colleague helped me to the car, I remembered where I was and I realised it was the end, just not for me.

***

Since that first incident with the truck driver, I've been very careful about limiting the amount of time I spend with the drivers to help avoid suspicion. Interestingly, I've met and spoken with one Lithuanian cattle-truck driver a number of times but he never remembers me from the previous encounter. I've used a variety of cover stories. The first time we met was in Northern France, at a service station just outside Calais. I was suited and booted with a generic, official-looking ID tag around my neck and a clipboard in my hands. I told him I was an EU inspector and he needed to hand over his paperwork. To my delight, despite seeming pretty annoyed about me taking up his time, he handed it over. A few snaps with the camera and I knew that, even if we lost him on the road, we could catch up with him at his destination and would therefore be able to document the animals' journey from beginning to end. Getting this paperwork on the road is hugely valuable to an information-gatherer working on behalf of animals.

In Europe, all animal exporters are required to submit a journey plan to the Agriculture Ministry in the country of origin in advance of transporting livestock. As many campaigners will testify, it's not uncommon for the journey plans not even to match up with the requirements of the transport laws; the stops required by law for the animals to rest are regularly missing or shorter than required. Occasionally, sections in the paperwork are left completely blank, with no information at all. For some authorities, the sheer volume of animals moving from farms to distant slaughterhouses must put huge pressure on the administrative system, because there is a lot of rubber-stamping.

The last time I saw the Lithuanian driver was in Ireland. I was working on tracking down some cattle that were due to be exported. With me was my colleague, and fellow campaigner, Pru. It was one of the first few trips we did together trailing livestock trucks across Europe. Spending days at a time working undercover with one other person can be an intense experience, and knowing you can trust the person you're working with is essential. Going through these challenging experiences brought the two of us closer together. And, while trailing livestock trucks perhaps isn't the most conventional 'first date', a loving relationship slowly blossomed. We went on to trail more trucks, and make our way side by side into factory farms and slaughterhouses. We officially 'tied the knot' shortly before this book went to print.

The farm was barren and filthy; the cattle, covered in mud and shit. We drove past in our black rental car several times to make sure no one was around and, when we were sure the coast was clear, Pru dropped me outside one of the barns. But, as I walked across an open courtyard to where the cattle were being held, our Lithuanian friend appeared out of nowhere.

'Why you here? Private property. Out!' he said gruffly as he strode right up to me.

I was sure he was going to recognise me, but I had to try my luck.

'I saw an owl, a big one. You never see them in the daytime. It flew into that barn.' I pointed and started to walk that way.

'No, no. You go. No owl.'

I stopped. He looked at the gate, and back at me. Pru had driven away to keep a low profile and was waiting in a pre-agreed lay-by down the road. I began pressing the walkie-talkie buttons repeatedly in my pocket, sending the crackles and beeps that would alert Pru that I'd run into trouble and that it was time to come and get me.

'Where you come from? You walk?' he asked as he looked at me closely.

'Oh just… over there,' I waved my hand.

It was chucking down with rain and not the kind of day on which you'd take a stroll in the countryside. The driver was getting increasingly suspicious so I made a quick move.

'I can hear the owl! It's back over that way. Thanks anyway!'

I dashed back to the road where I could see the car speeding towards me. Pru slowed down as she passed and, as I turned to give the Lithuanian a little wave, I hopped in and was whisked away to safety. I gave Pru a wry smile. 'You'll never believe who I just saw…'

Drivers, too, are usually under pressure to get to their final destinations in the fastest way possible, which puts a strain on them and that strain is, in turn, carried over to the animals. Occasionally, I've undertaken assignments on the back of information from a driver-turned-whistle-blower, since sometimes these drivers are at their wits' end and prepared to talk with someone like me just to help bring the company they work for back into line. In hushed tones, they speak about all the little tricks their companies use to circumnavigate the laws: taking longer routes to save on tolls, or fudging paperwork.

'It's just me hauling the animals,' one driver told me. 'It's impossible for me to stick to the law.'

Often there will only be one person moving animals from A to B, making it impossible to stick to European regulations for HGV drivers' hours. Inexplicably, livestock drivers seem to be exempt from following those laws as part of some unspoken rule understood across Europe. Sometimes they just break the rules without fear of punishment, but at other times the drivers find ways around the rules.

'I carry another driver's digital tachograph smart card,' another driver whispered to me.

This makes it look like there is a second driver, so they're taking turns to drive and rest. Drivers end up exhausted by these journeys and, wishing they worked for companies that followed the law, they become whistle-blowers. Bizarrely, they seem unable to comprehend the stress, exhaustion and fear that the animals they transport endure at the same time.

Factory Farming in Miniature

'It's going to cost you one hundred and fifty-four thousand euros to build this factory farm.'

That's what the three Italians on the other side of the desk had told me, after an hour-long negotiation had taken place at their factory.

'For that price, you will get one cage system to house two thousand quail for egg-laying and another five cage systems to rear seventeen and a half thousand quail for meat,' Lucilla, the office administrator, exclaimed.

Wanting to commission a custom-built quail factory farm was one of the odder cover stories I had ever used. But it was a starting point to discover more about one of factory farming's lesser-known industries – quail – while also finding out exactly what it took to build a quail factory farm. Of course, to make this blag believable, I had to be seen to drive a hard bargain. I managed to get a 20 per cent discount. I figured that would hit their profit margin hard.

It would be at least six months before they could start the cage build. Once the main structures had been built at the factory, they would then send a team of technicians over from the north of Italy to install the system as well as to add the automatic feeders, drinkers and manure removal belt that would keep the system free-flowing.

With six months to spare, and a few weeks before I would need to sign a contract and put down a deposit, I asked them where I might be able to see a working example of their system.

'You should visit Marco,' Lucilla said while winking at me. 'He will show you everything.'

She scratched down his number on the back of their glitzy catalogue and waved me goodbye.

Those few weeks before I had to sign the contract would be

long enough for me to get behind the scenes of this industry, at which point I would let the deal fall through.

Before setting off for Marco's, I had a flick through the catalogue they'd given me. It was laid out in a very similar way to the manufacturers' equipment catalogues used in the laying hen and broiler chicken industries: with lots of technical and performance data set alongside images and illustrations of the machinery and moving parts. Then there was the image of the system in use. In this case, it was a five-tier cage unit with a wire mesh tray in front of each cage tier. On that tray sat little white-and-brown speckled eggs and, peering out from the cage bars above it, thousands of little quail.

It was factory farming, just in miniature.

I've no idea how many people know that quail is farmed, let alone factory-farmed. If you want to see quail, you have a better chance in a factory farm than looking for them in the wild. Quail are very dispersed across Europe and their reclusive behaviour makes them difficult to find. They also have a strong migratory instinct and many European quail winter south in the Mediterranean, even flying as far down as tropical Africa. While not listed as a threatened species by the IUCN (International Union for Conservation of Nature), they have their threats to contend with. First off, hunters seek to bring them back to earth with the help of a shotgun as they make their way to breeding grounds. The quail that make it through that aerial flak are increasingly returning to habitats on the margins of farmland, which are struggling to survive under the pressure of agricultural intensification and pesticide use.

***

Marco's farm was set at the back of a single-carriageway road. It was a rural area but not remote. There were farms and farmhouses all around bordered by their own set of drainage ditches. Every property was visible to its neighbours, so not the sort of place that needed its own neighbourhood watch scheme. Farmers notice everything in the countryside anyway.

Marco, though, didn't live on site. There was no farmhouse there, just one long, windowless shed and the usual alarm systems placed out front to warn off unwanted visitors. Beyond the roof outline, I could see the snowy tops of the Dolomites in the distance. It was winter but there was no escape south for the quail at Marco's farm. Every door and window was shut, except for one door that opened into a machinery area at the back. I decided to take a look but first phoned Marco to see how far away he was and how much time I might have alone.

'I can be there in five minutes,' was his response.

My hand was already on the door handle as he hung up. Five minutes wasn't long, but any time alone is always valuable on these assignments.

They really are little, was my first thought when I saw the quail. Little and *very* cute. Tiny enough that one could fit in your hand. The factory system looked just like the catalogue illustration but, in real life, it was dirtier and seemed all the sadder.

No animal should have to face factory farming but putting a flying bird in a tiny cage, and in the process rendering their wings completely pointless, seems a particularly cruel thing to do.

Three minutes had elapsed since speaking with Marco and I had around one minute of footage in the can so, rather than get caught, I returned to the entrance and waited by my car.

Marco turned up a minute or so later. He was a small and very animated man. He was dressed smartly and looking forward to watching a national football game later that evening with friends. Even so, he was happy to talk about quail and not just his own. One of the first things he told me was that he was part of a consortium of quail farmers. Together they owned quite a few farms in the area and a slaughterhouse.

The birds that I had sneaked a peek at were the egg-layers. There were 4,000 of them in that one room and they would live like that until they were five months old. Beyond that age, they still laid frequently but not in a large enough quantity to keep up with the production numbers the consortium required. Much like the laying hen industry, perfectly healthy quail are considered 'spent' at quite a young age and will be sent for slaughter. But cages used in the food industry never stay empty for long. Each week another batch of eggs gets incubated, sexed (identified as male or female) and the hatched females are then moved into cages ready to begin laying eggs when they are fifty days old. Marco proudly showed me the incubator and then a room with thousands of newborn quail that were hatching from eggs and falling onto a wire mesh tray ready to be caged. There was not a mother for all these chicks to be seen, just a carpet of broken egg shells.

The quail cages at Marco's farm were divided up into compartments. In each compartment, just 1 m (3.3 ft) wide, there were thirty females alongside three males to breed with. The birds in the cages looked very different from the footage I'd seen of quail in the wild. In their natural environment, glossy feathers bounce sunlight off their backs, and their inquisitive eyes search for flies and insects in the stubble of the fields. They are constantly on the move. Darting left and right, they are followed by their young, who are busy learning from their parents everything they need to sustain themselves.

There, in those dark cages, all they could do was look across to others in the same predicament. Their feathers were dull and patchy with plenty of pink skin on show. The worst areas were the female's backs where repetitive mounting from the males, whom they could not escape, had worn away any chance of their feathers returning in those bald spots. When their bodies pushed up against the cage bars, their exposed skin would rub against the metal, compounding their suffering.

I'd always thought of quail eggs and meat as luxury foods. They're often found in high-end restaurants and considered a delicacy but, looking at their living conditions, this perception couldn't be further from the truth.

'So quail eggs are a luxury product here in Italy, are they, Marco?'

'Oh yes, they are very sought after, especially at Easter when many people across Italy will buy them,' he replied.

'Do you think people would be surprised if they saw how they are reared?' I asked.

'Perhaps,' he said. 'I'm not sure about the quail laying the eggs but I don't think we'll be able to keep quail in cages for meat production for much longer. People don't like it.'

Marco waved his fingers at me to follow him. Sliding back another heavy metal door, we entered another room with more cages and more quail.

'These are the meat quail.'

The cages were the same but the quantity of quail inside each compartment was noticeably higher. It turned out there were more than double the number of birds here than in the cages for the egg-layers. There was minimal movement sideways and birds would have to forcibly push their way to the back of the cage if they were to access feed and water.

When we entered the shed, thousands of plump little quail frantically jumped in unison. Quail are well known to jump when afraid – when in a group it's an excellent way to quickly confuse a predator – but here they smashed into the cage roof with their heads. It was only designed to be an inch or so taller than the natural height of a quail. I felt awful for triggering that fear response but I was only following the instruction of Marco, who didn't bat an eyelid.

As Marco went over to check a feedline, I did some quick calculations in my notepad to try and work out the living area allocated to one quail in that space. I had to do it twice because I couldn't believe how little the area was: 9 cm x 9 cm (3.5 in x 3.5 in), about the size of a beer mat.

'Would you like a beer before you head off?' Marco asked.

Quail being forced to live in a space the size of a beer mat didn't seem like something I wanted to drink to, but I said yes; I wanted to see if I could get some more leads out of Marco.

Over a drink, Marco explained a little bit more about what system he felt would replace keeping meat quail in cages if consumers demanded it on animal welfare grounds. He only came at it from the consumers' perspective, not his own. He didn't personally view another system as something that could be better for the birds. It would be a hassle and an extra cost for him; and, even though he found the cage system the most efficient way to farm quail, he was smart enough to know that he'd have to follow the market like everyone else if he wanted to stay in this cruel business.

'A friend of mine will show you this other system,' Marco said while punching some numbers into his phone to bring up Pietro's details for me.

'Thanks, Marco,' I said.

'Now, do you want to come with me to see the world's best football team play?' he asked.

I hadn't watched much of the game since the professional football club I was with in the UK dropped me. I was only an apprentice but everyone I knew was expecting me to sign a contract with them. Instead, I was shown the door. I wasn't that upset. By my late teens, I had cut out eggs and dairy and, as the only vegan in the squad, I was often teased by the rest of the team about my beliefs.

'Another time, Marco, but *Forza Italia*! [Go Italy!]'

***

Two days later, I met Pietro. He was big and scruffy, not at all coiffured as Marco had been.

'Welcome, welcome, Ricardo,' Pietro said, greeting me in dirty dungarees that struggled to contain his belly.

I soon detected an air of one-upmanship about him.

'I produce significantly more quail than Marco does. I send over eighty thousand quail to slaughter each week.'

Walking around the site you could see this was a factory farm of two halves: one run down and in a state of decay; and the other shiny and new with thousands invested in renewable energy sources, one of which was a biomass plant to generate heat and electricity.

I was not surprised to see the quail weren't part of the shiny new improvements, although the constant breeding cycle did make them a renewable resource as far as Pietro was concerned.

As we walked towards the non-cage set-up for fattening meat quail, I kept stopping whenever I saw a closed door. A closed door in a factory farm is something I always want to open as part of my campaigning fieldwork. It tends to be the entrance to a place even a factory farmer might feel ashamed to show someone.

'Is this the cage system, Pietro?'

'Yes, but you have seen it already, haven't you?' he replied.

'Well, I'm interested to see the system here as well, as it's what I have a quote for to set up at home,' I replied.

He opened the door and thousands of flies came pouring out. Not even they seemed to enjoy living here.

After taking a moment to let the worst of the flies out, I

entered. I walked first over a step, then over the body of a dead quail left on the concrete. I didn't have to look hard to see more dead quail lying between the cage bars or strewn about the floor. And then there were those flies. They hopped over quail droppings as they fell through from the wire mesh floor and onto paper sheets placed below to catch them.

'The quail eat the maggots when they hatch from the faeces,' he said when he saw me staring at the flies – a strange attempt at justification for keeping animals in filth.

Swarms of flies are not an unusual sight on factory farms, but seem especially bad on quail farms. I visited one farm in Greece some weeks later with Pru. This was when she was still fairly new to investigations and it reminded me what a shock the sheer quantity of flies can be to the uninitiated. As we stood and talked with a farmer, flies landed and crawled across his face. He didn't flinch but I could see Pru fixating on the ones crawling near his nostrils, which flared as he spoke excitedly. Then the flies began to land on us. The farmer was too focused on telling me all about the antibiotic system they used to notice Pru's attempts to cover up the horror she was experiencing as they crawled across her face. Her eyes widened when one crawled over her lips, but I'd warned her to 'think like a farmer' and she knew that meant not reacting, no matter how bad the flies got.

Just an inch or so above the paper sheets where the flies were feasting were the feet of his quail. I could see some were swollen to quite a large size, making the birds look like they were walking with a flesh-coloured balloon attached to their feet. The condition known as 'bumblefoot' is quite common in birds raised in factory farms and is caused by a bacterial infection that enters the foot from a cut causing it to swell up with a pus-filled abscess.

While there was very little room to move, I could see that,

when birds did try to walk, they limped, not putting any weight on the feet that were swollen. I winced. It must have been so incredibly painful for them.

Perhaps Pietro saw me wince because he told me the birds were now old enough to be 'out of the danger zone'.

'What do you mean by that?'

'Up to fifteen days of age you have to keep a very close eye on the temperature. Get it wrong and you could find the birds have smothered themselves to death, trying to keep warm – I've had it happen here.' Pietro concluded by saying, 'Our mortalities run to 7 or 8 per cent here.'

I got my notepad out again to do the maths. With 32,000 quail in this one shed alone that would amount to more than 2,500 deaths, and in just thirty-two days, the age when they were killed. I doubt such high rates of mortality would ever be accepted for animal enterprises that allow public visits. If this factory were a wildlife park, it would get closed down with those kinds of statistics, but as it's for farm animals it's perfectly acceptable to the authorities to allow such high death rates. Farm animals just don't have the same level of worth.

I was wondering how much better life for a factory-farmed quail might be in the final shed? This was the reason I was here, after all.

Pietro opened the door and I saw thousands of meat quail huddled together on the ground. There were no cages, but this was no different from a standard intensive broiler chicken farm. As the light streamed in through the open door, a few quail launched into flight. Like missiles with a malfunction, they came crashing down into other birds straight after take-off. As I stood looking in from the outside, one landed suddenly by my feet.

I picked her up carefully with both hands and just held her. I could feel her little heart beating rapidly. I was reluctant to put her back inside, as she was so close to making a break for freedom, but Pietro's hard stare forced me into action. I bent down and placed her back down amongst the other birds.

'Sorry,' I whispered.

'This system is called *a terra*,' Pietro explained. 'It means "on the ground". I actually prefer the cage system because in here they lie on their own waste instead of above it,' he added.

Pietro, along with another farmer in the consortium, had been trialling this system for the past two years. He told me it had been good for their export market and then showed me one of the labels used on the final product. It described the birds as free-range, a term usually reserved for animals that get access to the outside, which these quail clearly didn't. The label's sales blurb also included a smattering of flattering marketing terms that illustrated how exclusive and luxurious a product it was.

'Sometimes I have to bulk up orders for "free-range" birds with extras from the cage system next door,' Pietro said, shrugging his shoulders.

I was a little taken aback by this sudden confession and by Pietro's stupidity at being so open with a stranger. In fact, I'd captured his admission on my hidden camera but I also took some photos of the label and its code number, which linked it back to this farm. If factory farming wasn't bad enough, I'd now discovered fraudulent factory farming. This was one filthy business.

***

I left Italy a few days later but kept on a Southern European track and arrived in Portugal, another one of the leading players in the industrial farming of quail.

There are towns in Portugal that not only factory-farm hundreds of thousands of quail but also celebrate with quail-themed festivals dedicated to the birds – or rather dedicated to eating quails. Though the festival wasn't scheduled for the time I was in the country, I imagined it might be a useful talking-point for getting me signposted to some of the local quail farms.

As I drove north of Lisbon, I passed only a few of Portugal's famous cork forests. Large parts of the country are now covered by eucalyptus trees which, despite their popularity for the paper industry and their use in the production of oil and resin, don't offer much for local flora and fauna. I imagined any quail living in the wild here might struggle in this non-native set-up.

With the tops of eucalyptus trees swaying in a gentle breeze and a perimeter fence of rusty tin panels, the first farm I found could have been straight out of an Australian farming magazine. It had been difficult to locate. The address from a local farming directory was slightly off, so I drove around in circles for a while ending up at several farms, none of which had quail. Ultimately, it was the quail that gave away its location.

The song of the quail is both beautiful and unique. It's said to sound a bit like someone quickly and repeatedly saying 'wet-my-lips'. You can hear one bird from a fair distance, but it was the sound of maybe ten thousand quail singing in unison that I heard as I drove by.

I left the car and walked on foot towards the sound. About half a mile down a dirt track, I came to a heavily bolted door and a CCTV camera looking down towards me from the top of a telegraph pole. I peered through a gap between the door hinges and could see the long shed where the quail were housed. There were also six dogs running towards the gate.

If the owners hadn't spotted me on the CCTV, the barking of the dogs was surely going to make them aware that they had company. I looked up at the camera and gave it a wave, then petted some of the dogs that had managed to get their wet snouts through some holes in the fence panels. I peeked over the fence and caught the curtains twitching in a small block-work house. There was someone inside but they had decided they were not coming out and therefore I wasn't going in. I returned to the car, all the time accompanied by the beautiful quail song, a song that wouldn't be kept prisoner despite the confines of the singer.

The next few days proved much more successful. I managed to get in with some marketers associated with one of the big brands of quail and that helped me get a look at both the cage systems and the barn system that I'd also documented in Italy. The company used contract farmers to raise their meat quail for them, a bit like the system used in the USA to produce meat chickens. The farmers take delivery of day-old chicks, rear them, and return them back to the company when they are due to be slaughtered. Most of the meat birds are slaughtered when they are between twenty-eight and forty days old and weigh between 120 g and 150 g (4.2 oz and 5.3 oz). However, due to the deluxe nature of this trade, baby quail can be slaughtered at just eleven days old to supply high-end restaurants.

I didn't see the slaughter of the eleven-day-old quail, but I did gain access to the main slaughterhouse to watch the process for the older birds. With a few minutes before the slaughter, I went to a toilet cubicle to check my covert camera was running OK. It had been playing up a bit and I was concerned it was close to a breakdown. I could do basic fixes on it and on that day that would have to do until I got home and could return it to the manufacturer for a full investigation. With the little red light showing that it was recording, I walked back into a room that had suddenly become busy again with workers returning for a second shift.

I moved to the unloading bay and spoke with a manager.

Yellow crates, or modules as they are known, were stacked up in front of me full of live quail. Behind them, two women worked quickly taking the birds out of the modules and fastening the quail feet up into the shackles. Their wings flapped frantically.

'Here they are,' the manager said triumphantly.

He'd pulled some quail out from a crate and sat them like prizes on top of it so he could point out the finer details of their breeding.

'I love the striping across their backs and their little white chins,' he said.

Facing an open door, they sat slumped and dazed on the crate. If they just had the energy, they could have flown out of the door. I willed them to take flight but it was too late; a burly woman scooped them up in her arms and proceeded to secure them to tiny shackles dangling high up from a metal line. That was where hundreds of quail would be hung upside down by their feet. I heard the machinery cranking into action and the shackles began to move slowly.

I walked down the line. The first shackles came round empty, except for the gruesome sight of some little quail feet that remained stuck in the shackles, torn away from the animals' bodies earlier that day. Then came the first birds.

Above my head, the fully conscious birds hurtled past. It was not their wings propelling them forwards but the appetite of people. For the first time in their life, they were properly flying. They were also heading south, as they should have done on their migration. You see, these birds were going to be exported to Africa, one of the key export markets for Portuguese quail. I decided not to share that irony with the managers, partly because it would probably be lost on them; and, secondly, because I found it so incredibly sad that these birds would indeed end up in Africa but on a piece of styrofoam and in a cellophane wrap.

Moving further along the line, I watched the birds as they were stunned. Their heads were dipped in a water bath through which an electrical current passed. Some quail missed the bath by raising their heads up at the last moment. I watched one go through the neck cutter fully conscious and then had to look away and get my emotions back in check. There was no room for tears.

I had been fixated on the birds but, when I reviewed the footage later, I heard the manager talking about how healthy it was to eat quail meat and eggs in Portugal and how that was emphasised in the marketing messages of the business. He also spoke about how delighted he was to have seen red meat consumption linked to increased cancer rates and that was good news as far as he was concerned, as more people would look to eat quail products instead. I'm not sure how cancer could ever be considered good news.

But then he spoke about how antibiotics are added to the water supply for the first three days of rearing to avoid high mortality rates. Quail meat and eggs might be healthy for people in their view but the quail are brought up in the unhealthiest of settings. Dishing out antibiotics to all animals as soon as they are born is surely a sign that their own system must be sick.

***

Sitting at the airport waiting for a flight to Athens for the final part of this project, I received a call.

'Ciao, Ricardo. This is Lucilla.'

'Oh, hello,' I replied.

'I'm sorry but the timeline we gave you will have to change.

We have a build ongoing in the Middle East that needs more time to finish.'

I pushed for more information about the project.

'The quail are bred to feed the falcons,' she added.

It hadn't occurred to me that quail reared in factory farms might not be for human consumption. Falcons are the stars of a multimillion-pound racing industry. Falconry, a sport of kings, is a huge attraction, not just for locals but also for tourists flocking to the region to escape the cold, damp winters of Northern Europe.

How tragic that thousands of quail would have to suffer in cages, while another type of bird gets to fly and is lavished with attention by owners and gamblers alike for its speed and grace. I've travelled all over the world documenting the welfare of thousands of animals for lots of different organisations, and you never know where the next investigation might come from so, with my interest piqued, I asked them one more question.

'Where exactly did you say this was again?'

The Kill-Buyers

Americans love their horses – don't they?

The country was practically founded on horseback. Native Americans measured their wealth by them, the pioneers couldn't have settled in the Wild West without them and, of course, they did the legwork in helping the country create its first postal service, the Pony Express. Where would the cowboy be without his horse? The world over recognises the cowboy as an American symbol but, without his horse, he's just a man in a hat.

Horses can live for more than thirty years and so their lives often take several twists and turns. I was investigating one of those twists and, in turn, what I found was deeply troubling. I think America is falling out of love with its horses – if it ever truly loved them. And while it didn't take an undercover investigator to establish how some horses are treated – electric prods and flank straps (also known as bucking straps) are approved for use by the Professional Rodeo Cowboys Association[1] – I needed to delve into a darker aspect of the country's use of horses to find out more.[2] It is a business that, perhaps unexpectedly, turns tens of thousands of horses into hefty steaks for the restaurants of Europe and Asia.

My assignment in the USA was to gather evidence and document the trade in horses between the USA and the slaughter-houses of Mexico and Canada. In the five years leading up to 2017, it's been reported that more than half a million horses[3] have been trucked across these two borders to be killed, canned and exported to countries like France, Belgium and Japan.[4]

To begin with, I needed to find a place where horses were

1. https://bbc.in/2YuRZap
2. http://bit.ly/38jSJDI
3. http://bit.ly/34Ui7Oe
4. http://bit.ly/2Roy3V6

sold. From there I hoped to pick up a trail, which I believed would take me all the way to the gates of the slaughterhouse.

With a bit of pre-trip research, I soon learned that most of the deals for slaughter horses were done through the weekly horse auctions that take place on the edge of farming towns right across the USA.

They are popular events for the local community; a gathering place for old farm hands to 'chew the cud' and for young kids to pick out their first pony. At the largest sites, local crafters sell their wares like jams, chutneys or cinnamon buns under small gazebos while others offer vintage clothes from dumpster-diving trips. They are pretty eclectic places, but in the shadow of all that merriment, parked up away from all the family hatchbacks and SUVs, are the livestock trucks. Big cabs, pulling long aluminium trailers, they wait at the back of the horse pens until the public has gone home. Only then do they load the horses they've bought at the auction. These are the trucks that belong to the people known simply, and ominously, as 'kill-buyers'.

In the end, I got very familiar with these folk, but at first, they were hard to find.

***

Starting out in California, I went to an evening sale of an auction not far outside of Los Angeles. I sat in city traffic for most of the afternoon, surrounded by Toyota Priuses, the people's choice for a trusty steed in these parts, and wondered how on earth this city could be part of such a trade. On the way, I scoured the traffic but saw nothing that was carrying a horse or even connected to horses. I was beginning to have my doubts. But, sure enough, those doubts proved unfounded when I turned into the parking lot of my desti-nation and it was crammed full with horseboxes and trailers.

'Welcome, friend,' said an upbeat guy.

'Hi,' I said as I left the parking lot.

When I was new to a place or campaign, I'd try to keep a

low profile and just quietly observe to see what I could learn. It helped me prepare for the next stage of my assignment and decide what investigative approach I'd go with. That wasn't always easy within the super-friendly and outgoing communities you often come across in the USA.

'Have a good day,' I added, my default response to close a conversation quickly.

Inside, the auction had a bit of a party vibe going on and, while there was plenty of double-denim on show, there wasn't a Stetson in sight. It didn't feel right. It was too jolly for kill-buyers, surely. But with its relatively close proximity to the Mexican border and some of the slaughterhouses that keep the cogs of this business turning, I couldn't rule anything out.

As the sun dunked itself below the horizon, the floodlights of the auction turned on and bathed the whole place in a smoggy orange. I watched people line up at a small kiosk to get information about what was on sale that night. A letter board sign hung at an odd angle, next to the kiosk window, with most of its letters missing. It looked like some kind of cryptic crossword. In the end, I deciphered that the auction was not, in fact, 'once a moth', but once a month.

Out back, I counted about forty horses. They were kept penned in a dusty courtyard. The boisterous horses were held individually, while those more on the docile side shared a pen. There were a lot of families here. Kids ran around loose, racing from pen to pen hoping to find their new pony. Behind the kids came the mothers. They buzzed about looking the horses up and down, before running a soft hand down their noses. They didn't try to stop their kids running amok with their frenzied screams and squeals that startled the horses, but they were the only people I saw showing any tenderness to the horses that night.

I listened in on a few conversations. First, a woman on her phone to a friend saying that the horse she was looking at had a leg injury.

She was right, the horse hovered one hoof slightly off the ground. I hadn't noticed but her keen eye had been here before. She wasn't a kill-buyer, though. Her tone was compassionate. She liked horses, you could see it just by the way she gazed longingly at the beautiful creatures. Her eyes followed the contours of the horses back from mane to tail and then back again. Would she take her? Perhaps, I hoped.

Another lady busied herself running hay to the horses. Initially, I thought she was a worker but, no, she cussed and tossed her hand back and forth, angry that the horses had no feed. She was right, there was no sign of hay except that which she was handing out to the horses. Auctions don't go in for full board. They're trading places, where animals pass through in a day or so and, as such, many animals are denied food and sometimes water. A few of the horses were thin and would have benefited from a good meal.

On the far side of the courtyard, I noticed a real Black Beauty of a horse. But she appeared disturbed. She was swaying from side to side and making repetitive movements with her feet as if she were Irish dancing in the dirt. A woman who stood alongside me was also struck by the disturbing behaviour.

'She'll be from the track. A racehorse that didn't make the grade,' she said.

The horse was a cast-off, no good to her former owners. I'd been told that many racehorses and ex-rodeo horses end up at auctions like this and it's not uncommon to find them in a kill-buyer's pen. Some are rescued but most end up on a foreign plate after passing through the auctions. Unlike animals raised to become food, horses used in entertainment are often carrying residues of anti-inflammatory drugs or antibiotics to help them recover from injuries. One anti-inflammatory, known informally as 'bute', is said to be used by 85 per cent of US horse owners but is a recognised lethal carcinogen in humans and as such is banned completely in food production.[5] But because regulations on this industry are inherently weak, those kinds of drugs can often pass through into the human food chain without getting picked up. One scientific report from 2010 said that there was no way to track bute entering the food chain, but that its presence is highly likely.[6]

A little later, I followed Black Beauty to the auction ring. A rider had just finished showboating on a horse by way of a few rodeo moves. It had got the bidders excited but made that horse edgy. Black Beauty was also tense and her ears flicked quickly from side to side as she was ridden up and down a narrow strip of dirt. It took just a few moments for the hammer to go down. I was expecting her to go for a lot more than $165, but that was all she raised. I followed the buyer, a middle-aged Hispanic guy, out to the parking area. Half expecting to see a big truck containing twenty-plus horses, I was relieved to see him load her into a small trailer, and then disappear into the night. He was no kill-buyer, but who knows what fate lay ahead for her and whether she was just on her way to a bigger collection station.

Soon after, I left the auction. I was looking for the big trucks and there were none outside that night. I decided to head somewhere where horses were a bigger part of the community. I drove straight to the airport and picked up a ticket that would take me not just to the American Midwest but straight into the heart of horse country.

***

The horse country of Indiana was pleasant. It felt like stepping back in time. Rolling fields and roads cut through pretty, wooded glades. I passed over historic, covered bridges that spanned sparkling creeks. And, as expected, there were horses, lots of horses. They munched at lush grass in generous paddocks, bordered by white

5. http://bit.ly/34XcNJK

6. Dodman et al. 2010. 'Association of phenylbutazone usage with horses bought for slaughter: a public health risk.' https://www.ncbi.nlm.nih.gov/pubmed/20176071

picket fences. It looked the way most people probably imagine life is for most horses in the USA.

But that picture didn't last. As I travelled deeper into horse country, the cars thinned out and the roads transformed into highways for horse-drawn buggies. Now it really felt like stepping back in time. The Amish community use horses to maintain a life free from modern-day conveniences. Shunning cars, and any oil-driven engines, the term 'horsepower' took on a more honest meaning here. The horses were forced to trot at a pace that at times bordered on a canter, and I was surprised at the speed they would travel. On one stretch of road, a buggy pulled out behind me. I slowed down and in my rear-view mirror, I could see the buggy keeping pace behind me. I pulled over to let it pass. The chestnut-coloured horse was soaked in sweat, mouth agape and nostrils flaring. The heavily bearded man riding up on the carriage yelled out at his horse. I couldn't hear his words, but the tone was angry. Even as they rode out of sight, I was left with the sound of hooves pounding asphalt in my eardrums.

Horses are integral to life in the Amish communities but they are for work, not pleasure. And over the next few days that became increasingly clear. The horses I'd seen pulling the buggies were standardbred racehorses. Those used to plough the fields are the heavier draft horses that are bred for farm work. I found both when I arrived at the auction the next day.

As I made my way to the auction area, I passed through parking lots where Amish buggies and their horses were tied up to pillars. The older men, dressed in simple white shirts, dark trousers and straw hats, kept themselves busy with their tack. Meanwhile the women, in their muted dresses and white bonnets, made their way to the flea market to sell their wares. They scuttled across the ground keeping their heads down. Keeping a low enough profile not to draw attention to themselves, they'd make good undercover investigators in the Amish world. A cover story for another day, perhaps.

Also working at the auction were Amish teenagers. With bowl-cut hairstyles, jeans and light-blue shirts, I found them ushering the animals out of the trailers. Like teenagers anywhere, they were laughing and joking and not taking their work very seriously. But one, in particular, stood out. He talked to himself while simultaneously screeching at his co-workers. He used very excessive force to unload animals into the market and, even though adults were around, he was never told to change his behaviour.

The 'loose horses' – a less inflammatory term given in these parts to those horses that would be destined for slaughter – hadn't yet arrived. So I followed the Amish kid for a little while in his work. I made my way up to an overhead gangway used by buyers to look down on and suss out the stock, and hit 'record' on my camera. My jaw almost dropped into the pen below, as the kid launched a full-blown mixed-martial arts assault on a goat that was giving him the runaround. Like a dervish, he whirled around landing kick after kick onto the face and body of the poor animal. I was stunned and gripped the camera tighter. This was evidence I couldn't miss. He then began using his hands and fists, not just in violence, but also to make offensive gestures at the goat. A couple of times he missed the goat and ended up in a crumpled mess in the dirt. Of course, this made him angrier and, with no one else around in this part of the auction, the goat then faced the brunt of that anger. This process lasted several long minutes. I'd never seen anything like it and more than once drew breath to shout down and tell him to stop. But I knew that if I left without that film – which would, without doubt, have been forcibly removed from me once I alerted the workers to my presence – this kid would be allowed to carry on practising martial arts on many more animals. I'd been tested like this many times, and I knew I had to sit tight, gather evidence and use it to try to effect lasting change.

Eventually, I was informed that this kid was fired after my investigation went public.

***

Horses had begun to arrive. I can only describe the way they entered the sheds as akin to injured troops making their way back to safety from the frontline of war. But this was not a place of safety. Big Belgian draft horses limped in, unable to match the speed at which the workers wanted them to move. Then came a series of horses, each with significant injuries: a cut eye on one filly, another with a big gash across the cheek, raw against its dappled grey coat. Next came the blind and the malnourished, some with ribs showing prominently; and, finally, the ponies.

Mostly, they were working horses that had been run into the ground in the farm-based communities. No longer fast enough to pull a buggy, no longer strong enough to drag a plough. Some, it seemed, were hardly strong enough to stand. But the ponies had not been worked. They came from a different place. They were once the pride and joy of little girls and boys, but those children were no longer little. The ponies had been outgrown, perhaps replaced by the next size up, and were no longer wanted. I can't imagine kids like that having any idea of what happens at auctions like these, but the only road for the unwanted ponies at auction is the one with a dead end.

The horses and ponies were tightly crammed into a couple of pens, in amongst animals they'd never met. Some lashed out at others with their hooves or teeth. They were clearly stressed – that aggression comes from fear.

Standing alongside the exhausted animals, I turned my attention upwards to the public gallery. It was there that I saw the serious buyers. Like vultures they circled over the auction ring, only stopping to perch together on the benches of the back row when the auction was about to start. The buyers used subtle gestures to signal a bid, and it was only the auctioneer who recognised their little ticks: a scratch of the ear or a yank of their cap. It took just a few minutes for several truckloads of horses to be auctioned off. They all went, including the ponies. Some sold for as little as $50 each. Any horse can end up in the back of a kill-buyer's truck.

After the sale, a worker came by and slapped stickers on their backs. A sticker signified that they were for slaughter. Those horses heading for better lives – not to Canada or Mexico – got a sticker placed on their tail. There were just a handful of those.

I had set up and concealed the camera in my car's back window earlier so by the time the trucks were ready to load, and the last of the public's cars had left, there would be no obstruction to filming. Then I waited. I planned to sit in the driver's seat, with an American Travel Guide and a notepad for my props. Should someone ask why I was sitting there, I could reel off a well-rehearsed story to deflect their nosiness.

I kept an eye on what was happening behind me from my car's rear-view mirror, which I'd angled in the same direction as the camera. When I saw something of interest, I jotted it down in my notepad, to make sure nothing significant got lost in the editing process later.

I gasped as horses were whipped up loading ramps or zapped into submission with an electric goad, which was thrust at a horse's hindquarters or even at their anus. They left the auction in the same way they had entered it – forcibly bullied into the back of trucks. Some, with heads down, accepted that abuse, while others challenged it with as much force as they could muster, rearing up and digging their hooves into the dirt. The weaker horses, those that were lame or malnourished, were treated no differently. The kill-buyers I saw showed no compassion for the needs of the individual. The horses seemed to be just meat to them, valued by the pound and not for their riding potential.

I set about trailing one of these metal monster trucks. Taking a few moments to set up another camera neatly on the dash-board, I followed the trailer across the state line. Not long after crossing, it slowed, indicated and made a wide, sweeping arc as it turned into the fuel station.

I waited for the driver to leave the cab, set the pump in motion and then go into the kiosk before I got out of my car. Watching his movements as I crossed the forecourt, I hit 'record' on my camera, sidled up to the back of the truck and peered inside.

Twenty horses were wedged in tightly, hooves scraping frantically against the metallic floor. They were still unsettled, heads flailing up and down. With my face pushed up hard against the aluminium sides, straining to look for injuries, I felt the powerful shocks that reverberated first through the metal, and then my face, as the horses kicked out desperately against their confinement.

'Is that aluminium?' a voice said.

I turned to see a two-tone blue uniform and shiny badge standing alongside me.

The police officer had a cheerful face with a big, fat walrus-like moustache. He seemed to think I was the driver and, for some strange reason, was curious about the trailer – not what was in it.

'Yep,' I said.

'How many can you haul at a time?'

I'm not really sure why I went along with it, especially given that the driver was in the gas station.

'Twenty,' I said, quickly concealing the camera in my jacket pocket.

'That's great,' the police officer said, his radio crackling in the background. 'Duty calls, have a great journey.'

The truck driver was getting close to the cab, so I walked

around to the back of the truck where I would be out of sight and then back to my car only once I'd heard his door shut.

The truck was heading in a slight northerly direction so it looked like a trip to Canada, not Mexico. I'd heard that in Mexican slaughterhouses the horses are left to bleed to death after a sharp knife severs their spinal cord. In Canada, they could expect a bullet to the head.

I lost the truck in the darkness. I was tired, which didn't help. Like the gamblers who'd once bet on racehorses running around the track, or the family who'd hoped that their pony might find a good home, I took a punt on where the truck was going from there. I drove on through the early hours, making short stops, which I guessed the driver might make to use the urinal or keep alert with a caffeine hit. My aim was to reach a slaughterhouse in Quebec by 5 a.m., a time when the workers would be arriving.

I passed by the Great Lakes and hugged the mighty St Lawrence River, before pulling up outside the slaughterhouse. Just a few moments later, the truck arrived. I hadn't seen it for eight hours but, sure enough, here it was. I already knew I wouldn't be going into the slaughterhouse. These people were very sensitive to cameras. A similar business had previously been exposed for poor slaughter techniques when a Canadian horse protection organisation received, and subsequently released, hidden camera footage from inside their slaughterhouse. All I could do at this point was document the horses' last slow and painful steps in this world as they were unloaded.

***

Returning to the Midwest, I planned to visit a kill-buyer's farm, or 'collecting station', as it was more formally known. I wanted to see what conditions were like for the horses on death row

– the place where they waited out their last days until enough horses had arrived to make up a truckload.

At the auctions, I felt slightly safer maintaining a level of anonymity amongst farm folk. But I knew that heading into a kill-buyer's premises would require a different approach. From my car I saw a paddock that ran alongside the state road in which stood an unusually large group of horses. Their heads were low to the ground nibbling the very shortest of sward as the sun beat down on their backs. In this world full of advertising, we become accustomed to blocking it out so, at first, I didn't register what was on the giant hoarding looming behind them: a 6 m (20 ft) cheeseburger stood over the horses, with those iconic golden arches alongside it. Though unrelated, it felt symbolic. Horses might not end up in a burger in the USA, but there's a good chance they'll be formed into a patty somewhere else in the world.

There was a barn at the back of the property where I could just make out the shadowy form of a horse. I wanted to get in there, but I couldn't access it from the front. It would have to be from around the back, where the railway tracks were. I parked up some distance from the farm and walked to the rail crossing, where the lights flashed and a barrier had gone down by the road. I saw an opportunity; the train could give me cover so that I could make the 200 yards along the track to the back of the barn completely unnoticed.

Running close along the side of a giant American freight train at full pace is not something I'd care to repeat. The gravel chippings were lumpy and uneven, sliding underfoot, and the space between the verge and the train was extremely narrow. As I ran, I imagined myself slipping, arms flailing, right into the mechanism of the train's wheels. I stumbled at one point and thought my heart might stop. Fortunately, it was just my camera that went crashing onto the unforgiving ground. This was not the kind of train that stopped and started. It was eating up the track as it sped across the Midwest to the East Coast. Having completed the 200-yard sprint I stopped, dusted myself down and waited for the rest of the train to pass by as I made a mental note to give trains a wider berth in future. Next stop, the barn.

It was a dilapidated place, with part of the roof falling in, though not enough to let in much light. To say the place was barren would be an understatement. Inside were several scrawny horses. They gnawed at the wooden troughs where there should have been food. Lips flared, their teeth grabbed at the wooden sides and pulled them back and forth, shaking the trough firmly enough for its fixings to rattle. The water buckets were empty, too. These horses were surviving, but hardly, with just enough food to keep them a few days and make it across the border. Clearly, it was not in a kill-buyer's interest to lavish horses with rich pickings when they would soon be dead. I left as quietly as I'd arrived, but only after topping up the water buckets. Sadly, without straying into open ground and risk being seen, I couldn't find any feed, only a tap. When given the chance, I'll always look to ease the suffering of an individual animal through this type of intervention. Unfortunately, those opportunities come few and far between.

***

I had one last auction to visit on my trip to the USA, and I was looking for a very particular type of horse. I'd been told that carriage horses sometimes ended up in the slaughterhouse. Carriage horses usually have a four-digit code engraved on one of their hooves, like a taxi's licence number. These numbers had, according to reports just a few weeks before my visit, been the tell-tale giveaway for a carriage horse that was found in the kill-buyer's pen at a notorious horse auction.

The carriage horse industry works hard to distance itself from the horse slaughter trade. However, there have been several high-profile instances of alleged carriage horses being rescued from a loose horse sale or a kill-buyer's truck.[7]

***

Horses don't normally peer out of third-floor windows. But, let's face it, there are a lot of crazy things going on in cities across the USA. In the heart of one city, I stood at street level gazing up at a series of small holes in a brick wall. Long faces looked out, not onto lush paddocks, but onto the high-rise cityscape. It was odd, surreal even, to see them living like this. I wanted to document what life was like for them after a long shift pounding the streets pulling a carriage behind them so, when the coast was clear, I walked into the stables through the same wide entrance the carriage horses would use to enter and exit the stables.

Inside it was quite dark. I found some horses confined to narrow tie stalls, tethered to their troughs with chains. There didn't seem to be much sawdust on the floor, and I felt it couldn't be offering them much comfort.

One of the biggest public concerns about the use of carriage horses in city centres is how unsuited the carriages are to sharing roads with heavy traffic. A legal report from one US city lists thirty accidents in a ten-year period.[8] When I visited, there was pressure on several cities to ban their use.

I spoke to one carriage horse driver and asked him about his experiences in the traffic. He was quick to tell me his story.

'My horse becomes very frightened in traffic,' he said. 'One

7. http://bit.ly/33PXVeP, http://bit.ly/2Lpx8jp
8. http://bit.ly/2sDvXX2

time he bolted and I fell off. I got caught up in the tackle and dragged alongside the wheel.'

'Were you OK?' I asked.

'I ended up in the hospital, so no, not really.'

'And your horse was OK?' I asked.

'On this occasion, yes, but the big trucks are very scary for him and also the large groups of people that crowd round using flashes on their cameras.'

I thought that was telling. Horses were never going to escape tourists in the middle of a bustling metropolitan city.

On foot, I followed some of the drivers around the city and watched them weave precariously through the traffic. For the horse, as a prey animal, sight is an extremely important sense. Horses can see round an incredible 350 degrees but put blinkers on and that can be restricted to as little as 40 degrees. When working, carriage horses are permanently fitted with blinkers to keep them looking firmly ahead and a little sheltered from the chaos around them. If the only way to make a horse function in a city is to fit them with restrictive blinkers, then you've already taken a horse deep into an environment where it absolutely should not be. Once in the relative calm of a green space or pedestrianised area, the horses stand, waiting for customers from mid-morning through to late evening.

It's a long shift, and I didn't want to think about where it might end.

Last Christmas

I'd never had to kick the door open from the inside of a car before.

It was minus 25 degrees Celsius and, after eight hours of searching for a herd of reindeer in the Arctic, the doors of my hire car had jammed solid with cold. At times like these, the deposit you put down on a hire car seems unimportant. You just want a reliable vehicle. So, I leaned back, brought my knees up to my chest and double-kicked with as much force as I could muster. The door opened.

I climbed out and stood on the highway. In two hours not a single car had passed me. There was no point in pulling over, so the car sat stationary in the middle of the road. It was barely recognisable as the black car I'd hired in Kiruna, Sweden's northernmost town. Now, it looked like an ice sculpture in an art gallery. This wasn't a place you'd want to wander far from your car. It was hard to tell what was road and what was not; everything was a white-out. At just 3 p.m. it was getting dark and it was silent, so incredibly silent. After I'd managed to turn the car round, I headed back to town where I was staying.

That day had been a write-off in my pursuit of the Sami reindeer herders. But I had learned a valuable lesson. I was going to need help from a local if I was to find the reindeer in this vast tundra.

The Sami people have inhabited Arctic Europe for the past 5,000 years. They're well known for their semi-nomadic and traditional lifestyle. Reindeer have historically been an important part of their culture and countless documentary-makers have filmed the beauty of sweeping herds of reindeer in the snow with their young calves clumsily bumbling around like Bambi.

My assignment was to try and document the darker side of reindeer herding. I'd learned that every year tens of thousands of reindeer[1] are herded and trucked to commercial slaughter-houses to meet a demise that is anything but traditional. Essentially, I wanted to take the tour that visitors never took. The tour that didn't include sleigh bells or jingly music. The story of what happens when the TV wildlife crews have packed up and gone.

***

The following morning, there was even more snow. Dense, heavy flakes were slowly dropping from the grey sky that rules here until the spring thaw. I had a quick breakfast, put on my coat, hat and snow boots and began the search for answers.

But getting out of the house I was renting wasn't as easy as I'd thought. When opening the door, I was confronted by a wall of snow. The overnight wind had driven it into the doorway where it had forced itself up against the door. I took a shovel to it and spent the next thirty minutes clearing myself a path to the outside and then a further thirty minutes walking into town through deep snow that the plough hadn't yet cleared.

The town was typical of the small communities that call the far north of Sweden home. It felt like the wilderness could swallow up this neat and compact place whenever it wanted to. The main focal point was the cultural museum, closely followed by the pizza place. The only person I saw was smothered in clothes and walked away from me into no-man's land. They pulled their shopping on the back of a small sledge and walked with purposeful confidence that put me to shame. Nothing else was moving.

I kicked off the snow from my boots and entered the cultural centre. It was bathed in warm orange light, and reindeer skins

1. https://www.ncbi.nlm.nih.gov/pmc/articles/PMC5549279/

hung from the walls. There was no one there except for a woman in her sixties, who sat quietly at a desk. Her head was buried in a newspaper.

'I'm looking for reindeer,' I said.

'Well, you've come to the right place.'

We both looked at the skins, and then back at each other.

'I'm looking for live ones, actually,' I said. I flashed my press card. 'Is there a reindeer herder I could talk to about the traditions of keeping reindeer?' I asked hopefully. With global television crews regularly visiting the region to document the Sami way of life, including the significance of the reindeer, it wasn't the sort of question that would raise suspicion.

'Yes, there is someone I know who would talk with you. She will be busy at the moment as they are preparing to move the herd.'

'That's great. Could I have her number, please?'

The lady scribbled down a number on the front of a brochure, which she probably gave to most visitors. She then weighed me down with every other tourism pamphlet they'd ever printed, even the Japanese versions.

Alongside the number she had given me was written the name Helga. I wasted no time and phoned Helga from my burner phone, a prepaid, cheap flip-phone topped up with credit on a cash-only basis. It wasn't traceable and I used it for all my investigative assignments.

It turned out Helga was happy for me to drop by her place for a chat there and then, so I headed back to my car to make the short journey to her home on the edge of town. Helga had long blonde hair. Her features were sharp, as if they'd been sculpted by the extreme weather.

'Come in out the cold,' she said.

'Thank you. It sure is cold up here.'

She was welcoming and invited me into her trophy room of

reindeer memorabilia. It was her lounge but it felt more like a shrine to taxidermy. There were a few family photos dotted about but they felt lost amongst the mounted antlers and skins draped across the furnishings. She didn't offer up a seat but I sat myself down at the table, hoping to buy a bit more time.

'I'd like to document the tradition of herders bringing reindeer down to their winter grazing lands,' I said, hoping to plug the gaps in my knowledge with hard facts. 'Can you tell me what that will involve?'

'We will examine the herd, identify our own animals and earmark those who will be slaughtered, particularly the calves born earlier that year.' Helga was a tough, no-nonsense type and as such our conversation was cordial but quite matter-of-fact. It didn't last more than a few minutes. 'Here are the coordinates for the reindeer gathering,' she said. 'We will be moving them down from the mountains to this place the day after tomorrow. They're not all my reindeer but you can expect to see about four thousand.'

Helga didn't ask what TV station I was with, or where the rest of my crew were. It seemed getting her name from the cultural centre was reason enough for her to speak to me. However, she was busy and needed to run an errand so I put my coat and gloves back on, thanked her for her time and left.

As I pulled out onto the main road, a large livestock truck lumbered up to the traffic lights. With a grumbling engine and a few puffs of dark black smoke, it stopped. It was empty but, with no other livestock in this region, I reckoned it must be being used to transport reindeer, so I switched lanes and pulled up behind the truck to see what I could learn. I had to be careful, though. With such little traffic in the region, I didn't want to get noticed, so I followed at a distance on its journey north. I only sped up if my GPS showed an approaching junction. A last-minute turn-off is all it takes to lose hours of effort spent following a missing truck.

When you think of reindeer, they're usually pulling sleighs to the sound of an upbeat Christmas tune; and always with happy, joyful children. But this was a sad old truck, and thousands of reindeer must have taken a one-way trip in it. No jingles, no bells, no smiling children.

Exactly an hour later it pulled into a petrol station. I got out.

'Hej,' I said in Swedish.

Given Swedes often speak better English than the natives of the English language, I quickly reverted to that and asked if he was heading to pick up reindeer.

'No, I'm finished now. I dropped reindeer in Jämtland earlier today.'

Jämtland was a lot further south than where I was now.

I felt his mood was relaxed so I spent a few minutes with him telling him about my search to find herders bringing their reindeer to their winter grounds. His name was Bo and he helpfully gave me a few addresses of people I could talk to. When I checked these out later, some of them turned out to be owners of slaughterhouses. He'd actually finished hauling for the week but said he knew that reindeer herders were out in helicopters earlier that day looking for their herds so something should happen soon.

Helicopters are often used by herders to locate their reindeer. In most nomadic cultures, technology is increasingly being used to keep traditions alive. But I hadn't seen or heard any helicopters yet.

With the days so short, darkness was descending again. I said my goodbyes to Bo and got back into a warm car, the only friend I had around here. The small ice crystals that felt glued to the hairs on my face slowly thawed. I'd only been outside for ten minutes, yet nature had marked me.

***

The next day was another early start and I was determined to get some footage in the bag. I planned to check out the addresses Bo had given me but first I brewed some coffee. I can't function before I've had at least two cups of strong, dark bean and a hot drink makes all the difference in such a cold place. Working in sub-zero temperatures throws up some unexpected challenges, especially when it comes to vehicles. As well as breaking your way out of your car, you also need to charge your car battery overnight, just to keep your car functioning for the next day – the car's very own coffee hit.

It wasn't difficult to find the first address Bo gave me. It was a drab building on the edge of a small town. There were no obvious clues as to what it was used for but there were a few cars parked in a hard-standing area, so surely there were people about, somewhere. Rather than go in through the front door I headed to the back entrance instead. A large wheelie bin stood covered with a dusting of snow. I walked over and opened the big lid. Inside lay all manner of animal body parts, and at the top of the pile was the head of a large elk. His cold, dead eyes looked up at me. I took a little film, then stepped back to peer through a plastic curtain that ran the full length of the closed back door.

'Hello?' I called.

'Hello,' a man said, approaching me from behind. He was wearing white overalls, white boots and a white hair net that was struggling to stay fastened to the wild hair on his head.

'What are you doing here?' he asked in English.

'I was hoping to speak to someone about reindeer,' I replied.

'Well, you should normally make that request in writing to our head office,' Stefan said.

'Yes, I normally would do that, but I was in the area and thought I'd drop by, just to ask a few questions.'

'OK, I have a few minutes, what do you want to know exactly?' Stefan introduced himself as a supervisor and explained that he'd come across the Baltic Sea from Poland for work.

'So what happens here, Stefan?'

'This is just a meat-cutting plant, where reindeer and elk are "processed". Nothing is killed here; that happens at the slaughterhouse.'

It wasn't quite what I was looking for but, once someone has their guard down, there is always an opportunity to learn more about the subject you're investigating. I kept Stefan talking.

'The carcasses arrive here early in the week and then the workers – who are all seasonally employed – cut them up and put them in the freezer. They then get collected at the end of the week and shipped north to a distribution centre.'

At this point, Stefan invited me into the huge freezer, the kind that people get locked inside in horror films. Inside, hundreds of reindeer carcasses dangled from sturdy metal hooks across the full length of the room. A stamp marked SWEDEN was tattooed across every thigh.

'All reindeer meat products from across Lapland have the EU's Protected Designation of Origin status [PDO]. Having that prestigious status is the recognition that reindeer meat has been produced in the region where reindeers come from. It opens up a lot of overseas markets for our products,' said Stefan proudly.

I was soon to see at first-hand how these commercial export players had helped turn what was once an exclusive right of the Sami people into a business that broke from both tradition and the law. I knew PDO was a big deal within the food sector, and a big marketing coup for the reindeer meat industry, so I put on my best 'I'm impressed' face while Stefan concluded the tour. A few minutes, as is often the case on these assignments, became an hour. I thanked Stefan and let him return to his work.

I stood in the road outside the unit and searched for my car keys, which had become lost amongst the layers I was wearing. I had felt warmer inside their freezer. As I patted my pockets, I reflected on what I'd learned from Stefan. Although so far I had been unable to document reindeer slaughter, it was the first sign for me that reindeer were more than just a few meals for a Sami family. Judging by the size of this facility and its connections to the global food market, big business had the tightest grip on the reins when it came to using reindeer. To me, it was starting to look very different from the portrayal of reindeer as part of the Sami traditional way of life that I'd seen on nature documentaries.

***

Back inside the car, it took several attempts for me to type the other address that Bo had given me into the GPS. My fingers felt like they didn't belong to me anymore. Feeling frustrated, I turned the dial of the radio on just in time to hear Wham!'s 'Last Christmas'. It was only the end of November but I guess they never escape Christmas here.

The roads were straight and these ones had markers placed high enough above the snow to tell you what was road and what wasn't. They frequently passed over large rivers and lakes that criss-crossed these northern provinces. Beyond the roads' edges was one continuous strip of pine and birch trees. The blueberries and cloudberries had gone now, but their brittle stalks could still be seen poking out just above the snowline. A month ago, foreign workers would have been rampaging all over these bountiful lands, supplying global food retailers with their foraged produce. The same companies that oversee the 'wild berries' business are also involved in the reindeer meat industry. As winter sets in, they switch from gathering berries in baskets to stripping the hides off reindeer.

The snow had started to fall heavily again. With a side wind from the east piling in hard against my windscreen, I cut my speed right back just in time to pass a fully clothed man sitting on a sun lounger on the edge of the road. Yes, a sun lounger in the snow. For a moment, I was sure I'd been subjected to some kind of strange mirage.

I stopped the car, checked my mirror and, sure enough, there he was, still there. I reversed back, bringing the car alongside him and wound down the window.

'Everything OK?' I asked.

'Yes,' he said as if this was completely normal.

There was a rifle resting on his knees and his snow camo clothes were topped off with a fluorescent orange cap. A walkie-talkie crackled from his top coat pocket.

'What are you doing?' I asked, but it didn't take more than a fleeting glance to see he was a hunter waiting to kill.

'I'm hunting elk and you're disturbing me,' he said. 'Please turn off your engine, it's too noisy and will scare the elk.'

Thinking of the large elk head that had peered up at me from the bottom of the wheelie bin, I decided to keep the engine running. Back at the processing plant, Stefan had said that 3,000 elk a season pass through their processing plant, all shot by hunters. I wanted to try and reduce that number by one. I drove away and then back a few times, each time tooting my horn repeatedly and avoiding eye contact with the hunter, hoping it would scare away the elk that were being driven out from the forest towards the road by the person who would be on the other end of the walkie-talkie.

My work has always focused on trying to reduce animal suffering on a larger, and often intangible, scale. It's rare for me to be able to save an animal during these assignments. It's something my conscience struggles with. So, moments like these, when I can alter a situation so that an animal survives, are moments I treasure.

As I made my last pass, I checked my rear-view mirror. The hunter was shouting angrily as he stomped around his sun lounger. He could have taken a shot at me but, instead, he grabbed the orange hat from his head and angrily threw it. It caught the wind and flew back in his face.

***

The next place I visited was definitely a slaughterhouse. It took a bit of finding but a large truck had left tell-tale wide tyre tracks pressed into the fresh snow back at the junction. The slaughterhouse was hidden deep inside a dark forest and surrounded by pine trees. Their thin branches were struggling to take the weight of another dump of powdery snow that day. There was no place to park up and quietly wait and see for a while, so I had no choice but to enter the slaughterhouse straightaway. I didn't fancy getting caught fumbling around with my camera right outside the building, so I had switched it on at the first sign of those giveaway tyre tracks.

As I drove in, I'd caught sight of a large pen alongside the central building. It was crammed full with reindeer; noses down snuffling out lichen to feed on.

Armed with a notebook and pen, I walked boldly across to the main entrance. A worker passed me with a wheelbarrow of bloodied innards. I nodded at him but didn't stop for fear of getting delayed unnecessarily with a series of awkward questions. He nodded back and kept walking. At no point did I look back to check if he'd suddenly questioned my presence. Instead, I was moving decisively to the main door.

'Hi, Bo sent me,' I said to the receptionist.

Bo was a common name and the receptionist didn't think to ask me, 'Bo Who?'

Creating a dialogue with someone on the edge of an industry, like Bo, can be a vital ingredient in opening a pathway into a facility normally off-limits to the public. I wasn't yet in the slaughter zone but with a little bit more chit-chat, I thought I could get there.

'I'm here to see the manager,' I added to help out the receptionist, who was just staring at me.

'OK, wait here,' she said and disappeared out back.

Eric, the manager, had a very orderly office. We drank bitter coffee while he filled me in on the inner workings of the industry. I scribbled furiously, trying to keep up with every fact and figure he was happy to share.

'Fifty thousand reindeer will be slaughtered in Swedish Lapland this winter,' he triumphantly told me.

'What about across the border?' I probed.

'In Finland, it will be double that figure.'

'And what type of meat is most popular?'

'The meat of the calves, both here and for our overseas market. They are mostly five or six months old and usually males.'

I was silent. I couldn't react to that question knowing now that thousands of reindeer don't even live long enough to see Christmas. They're killed as infants, weighing just 21 kg (46 lb).

Eric liked the sound of his own voice. He was an encyclopaedia on reindeer and I learned a great deal from that meeting, including a few more names of people he suggested I meet with. While I have snuck into animal production facilities in the middle of the night, I much prefer walking into places in broad daylight, while they're fully operational. It could be considered a risky approach, especially when combined with hidden cameras, but it's one of the most effective ways to understand what day-to-day life is like in these facilities, not just for the animals, but also to document how workers interact with them and how they justify doing what they do. These moments of conversation with owners, managers and workers really have been vital components in my documentation of industries that use and abuse animals.

I was thrown a pair of overalls, some plastic shoe covers and a one-size-fits-all hair net. With a shaved head, I found the hair net a little surplus to requirements but did as I was told. I was taken to the processing line where we stood midway so I couldn't see inside the room where the reindeer were being stunned, the process of rendering an animal unconscious before they are killed. However, documenting the first stage of the processing line was very valuable so I set about that task. Unfortunately, the overalls covered the covert camera in my shirt, so all I was filming at that point were the strands of white polyester that held the fabric together. The vet, who by law had to be employed by the slaughterhouse to enforce food safety and animal welfare, was standing beside me. He told me this was the best slaughterhouse in the country.

I often get told that when I'm in slaughterhouses: 'This one is state-of-the-art...', 'We lead the way in this country...', 'This slaughterhouse is the best...' It's pretty depressing.

The vet stuck to me like glue, so I had to wait until he got distracted with a colleague before I could undo a couple of buttons on the overalls. Standing very still, I looked down the line where reindeers' throats were being cut, and showers of their blood were hitting the floor and splashing back on workers' boots. In the background, a radio was blaring out Swedish pop songs; for once, it wasn't a Christmas tune. Then the vet returned to my side. He'd noticed my overalls weren't done up fully so he gave me a look, which I could tell meant, 'do them up'. He then moved back to the end of the line. I moved to the front of it and undid the buttons again as I stepped over tides of blood seeking a drain to pour through. A few minutes went by, then he was back. He frowned at the undone buttons. I gave him my puppy dog eyes but it wasn't enough. The combined noise of music, machinery and animals was so loud that I had to use hand gestures to mime that the overalls were too small for me (they were too big if anything) and that's why they kept coming undone. He gave me a steady, sceptical stare.

'I'm heading out,' I shouted.

He nodded and got back to scribbling on his clipboard.

Everyone else seemed pretty relaxed or at least unconcerned by my presence. Experience has taught me that getting seen first with the on-site manager helps prevent other staff from questioning the reason a stranger is present in an otherwise secure area. Just walking in, in broad daylight, can result in an 'access all areas' pass, and as an undercover activist you can't ask for more.

I walked around the rest of the plant, nodding 'hellos' at the workers and smiling like the tourists do when they meet the look-a-like Santa Clauses peddling their 'ho ho ho's. I came full circle and ended back in the slaughter area. There was no sign of the vet, so I approached the stunning room. It was small, just a few yards square, with blood running down the steel walls. A young man was standing in there with ear defenders on. He was reloading his captive bolt gun with blank gold cartridges. In a few moments that gun would be against the forehead of a reindeer propelling a steel bolt into its brain to render it unconscious.

'Alright if I hop in?' I asked.

'If you like,' he replied.

I stepped over the aluminium gate, over which the stunned reindeer were hoisted on their way to the processing area. After the stunning, the reindeer's back legs are shackled before being hooked up to the hoist.

The slaughterman was called Bjorn and we exchanged a few words. He looked a little surprised that I wanted to join him in there, but he didn't question me. With 400 reindeer to slaughter that day he had no time to waste. I watched him drop the last cartridge into the gun's chamber and then walk through a small opening to the outside where the reindeer waited out their fate.

I moved into a corner of the room, where I would be obscured from the reindeers' view. I wanted to minimise their stress as much as I could. No sooner was I in position than three reindeer came skidding in and in their frenzy slammed straight into the back wall. Being separated from the herd is extremely stressful for these animals. Safety in numbers is a way of life for them. When they are taken away from the herd, their fear is palpable.

I hadn't expected three of them and suddenly the space felt very cramped. They were wide-eyed and their hooves slipped on the metal floor as they desperately scrabbled for a foothold. The antlers on one of the reindeer were already soaked in blood, possibly from an injury that occurred during their transport to the slaughterhouse. Bjorn wrestled with one reindeer by the antlers. The reindeer tried vainly to keep his footing as his head was pulled closer to the gun. I was transfixed by his hooves. They were scratching furiously at the floor as if trying to keep pace with a treadmill set too fast. Then one hoof gave way and, at that moment, he lost the little traction he had. A moment later, he lost his life too. But he had fought hard and it took multiple attempts before Bjorn could get the gun flush against his forehead. Without ear defenders on, the shot bounced around loudly inside my ears.

The reindeer slid slowly down the wall, his head facing

towards me. A large spot of blood now marked the area of soft grey fur between his eyes. Bjorn had already turned his attention to the other two and the same process began again. Now, with a little more room, the reindeer raced around, bouncing off the walls and into each other, but there was no way back to the safety of the herd. An antler sliced across my thigh and I felt first-hand the power of the reindeers' fear. Over the next thirty minutes, I documented the same panic, stress and pain of so many animals. It is inexplicable how these methods could ever be thought of as a humane treatment for these semi-wild animals. Yet this was the 'best slaughterhouse', I had been told. What would the worst one be like?

The contrast between a life of roaming wild lands free from the presence of people, and this bloody wrestling match, was stark. Bjorn was Sami but this was one job and one setting that surely broke with tradition. Sami herders have explained their relationship with reindeer as one where their 'souls touch, or better still, overlap'.[2] I just couldn't imagine a setting like this being part of that relationship.

***

The next day started early with a drive out to the herders' rendezvous point. The drive was uneventful, but I did stop once, to allow a little mink to run across the road. I hadn't seen any wildlife *in the wild* in this country yet, so she was a welcome distraction from the memories of the day before.

As is often the case with animal production, there was no one else around until there was everyone around. The road had come to an abrupt end in a supermarket-sized car park. Mini-trucks, pick-up trucks and trailers were spread out in no particular order and people were busying about, carrying ropes

2. https://www.survivalinternational.org/galleries/reindeer (slide 9)

and knives through knee-deep snow to an area beyond the car park.

That area was the battlefield.

I grabbed all my camera gear and waded through the snow to put myself in the heart of the battle. Reindeer, so many, were running as a herd in vast circles. Heat rose off their backs leaving trails of vapour in their wake. Take away the people and it would have been an amazing sight, but it was the herders who were driving this momentum, not the animals. With lassoes and ropes, they were singling out individual animals, both calves and adults, and grappling them to the ground by their antlers or necks. Once their force had been exerted and the creature was down, the herders sawed out a jigsaw piece of ear flesh to mark them out as theirs. Like branding, the mark is passed down through the generations and helps herders pick out their animals when they are grazing. In the aftermath, young calves with bloodied ears stood alone, calling out for their mothers.

Away from the main action and out of the corner of my eye, I'd noticed three men aggressively pulling an adult reindeer towards a small hut. With one end of a rope twisted around its antlers and the other firmly in the hands of the herders, they were inching him closer and closer to where they wanted him. Keeping well back, I documented its struggle and then the sudden moment when the knife came stabbing down into the back of its neck. I was horrified. This was a killing method prohibited under Swedish law but out here there were no government agencies present to ensure the rule of law was upheld. I realised that only my documentation, at that moment in time, would ultimately be the way that the rule of law could be enforced.

By this time I was filming openly, and it was becoming clear that this was a problem. Herders started to approach, challenging me with accusing fingers and pointing at my camera. I had to keep moving constantly between the groups of herders to stay safe. After leaving one group, I chanced upon a big truck with a double trailer. I hid my camera and went towards it. Nestled alongside the truck was a wooden corral and inside more reindeer and people were battling. While a man was sawing off the antlers of a live reindeer, a woman was shoving the other animals back. It was Helga. The no-nonsense woman was clearly exhibiting her power over the terrified reindeer.

The biggest vehicle on this site was here for her and it was obvious where it would be going next: the slaughterhouse. It's no wonder Helga had chosen to say nothing about this process when we met.

I peered in through the slats of the truck only for an antler to be thrust out. It missed my right eye by a whisker and instead got jammed between the slats. I intervened, pushing the antler back so it could right its head properly.

From my position, there was a good view across to the top of the loading ramp. I could see the reindeer were getting snarled up there. Those at the top were spooked and turning back. But they were meeting the ones coming up behind them who were being stressed out by the prodding and goading of the vocal herders. No one thought to take a calmer approach and slow things down so the deer could work out what to do. It was just a cacophony of noise. As a result, the loading took some time and the stress levels for everyone involved went up and up.

I remained for a while and stayed on the other side of the loading ramp to keep out of Helga's sight. Given the reaction of herders that day, she might not have approved of me filming this sequence of events.

When the truck was nearly loaded with anxious reindeer, I left and returned to my car where I could wait for it to pass on the main road. I then trailed it for a while but lost it in the darkness later that night. However, I was now close to the Finnish border and there was one place I still had to get to, so I crossed over into the neighbouring country. I drove for a few hours and then stopped at a service station for some sleep, and then some coffee, before continuing with my journey.

***

By daybreak, I was outside another slaughterhouse. It was much bigger than the Swedish one. It had to be, to deal with the throughput of a larger reindeer industry on this side of the border. It reminded me of some of the modern slaughterhouses built for cows and pigs that I had investigated in some of the world's most carnivorous countries.

This time, I didn't gain entry straightaway. It took a few meetings where I was told to go away and come back again later and then again, the next day. But a bit of patience was worth it and, eventually, they were satisfied that my journalist credentials were legitimate. Having got past their initial suspicions, I then got the full tour – well, the tour they had created for me that day.

I was told that nearly 90 per cent of the reindeer slaughtered here were calves and in just a few days would be on the plates of diners in the gourmet restaurants of Germany, the Netherlands and Belgium. When it came to viewing the actual slaughter, it was comparable to what I'd seen in Sweden but on a much bigger scale. There was a lot of blood. You would expect that in a slaughterhouse, of course, but at times my boots were completely submerged in deep pools and rivers of it. I'd never seen that before.

I had been filming covertly when Anders, who was leading me around, stopped. He ended the tour where, logically, it should have started, at the live reindeer holding pens. These pens were hidden from outside eyes, tucked away in the central part of the slaughterhouse, open to the sky but enclosed by walls. A section of one wall was made of wire mesh and it was there that Anders stopped to show me the reindeer. This was a shot I knew I needed to capture but the wire mesh came up just higher than the positioning of the button camera concealed in my shirt. If I was going to get a clear shot, I had to raise that camera a little higher up. As we watched the reindeer swirl in tight circles, I slowly shifted onto my tiptoes and puffed my chest up to get the right angle. Stood in this slightly odd posture, I felt Anders' eyes burning into me.

'Are you wearing a hidden camera?'

'No,' I said. 'Why would you say that?'

'Well, your posture is just a bit odd right now.'

He had me there. There was only one thing for it, I had to call his bluff. I glared at him with a look that said, 'How dare you!', and undid the top button of my shirt.

'You want to check me over?'

He said nothing, so I slowly undid another button.

I'd undone three buttons before he awkwardly blurted, 'No, it's OK. Sorry.'

One more button and he'd have seen the tiny camera suspended behind it.

It was a close call and I was feeling shaken, but I had to keep my cool and let things run their course. Before he had a chance to think about it much more, I returned to my cover story – an article about the rise of 'exotic meats' – and fired off a few distracting questions. However, the atmosphere between us felt different now.

From the reindeer pens, Anders took me to a glass-panelled room that overlooked the processing line. Anders shut the door and left me alone with a bear of a man. He didn't say anything to me. The Bear looked down at the processing line while I tried to work out what was going on. Was Anders calling the boss? Their security staff? The police? Maybe my bluff hadn't worked after all. As the minutes went by, I reassured myself that the next people to walk through that door would be law enforcement; rather that than someone to rough me up.

Instead, the next person to appear was Anders.

'Here, a present from us,' he said. He held a lump of raw meat as a gift, which just hours before had been part of a living, breathing, being.

The Bear grunted and said, 'You won't eat that. You love Rudolph the reindeer too much in your country.'

I looked down at the meat in my hand and said, 'Well, there's no red nose here, so I guess it's not Rudolph.' I laughed nervously with them. 'I should really get going. Thank you for your time.'

Once out of the parking lot, I pulled over and sat slumped in my car. My hands were shaking and, for once, it wasn't from the cold. I knew I'd sailed a little too close to the wind in there but I also knew that confronting suspicion head-on was my best chance of getting away with it.

***

My instincts paid off that time. Following this investigation, more than 65,000 people called on the Nordic Council to end the cruelty to reindeer. The methods of handling, transporting and killing reindeer documented in this investigation caused ripples through the country and amongst the Sami people. The County Administrative Board in the region, where much of the footage was filmed, and The National Union of the Swedish Sami People spoke out and made it clear that stabbing reindeer in the back of the neck must end immediately.[3]

3. http://bit.ly/2rY68Rb

I was ready to go home, but there was one last thing I wanted to see, and it was on the other side of town.

Just a ten-minute drive from the slaughterhouse, I'd found another commercial venture where reindeer played a central role. Here, families were queuing up to gain entry to a large Santa-themed amusement park where one of the main attractions were Santa's 'real life' reindeers. The laughter carried across to me and in through the car window and I could hear chatter in a whole range of languages from the excited tourists. I saw a small girl, smiling ear to ear as a curious reindeer snuffled at her hands for a treat.

As people greeted these beautiful animals with curiosity and respect, there was a real sense of happiness and joy.

Epilogue

This book marks the final chapter in my undercover journey for animals.

I never expected to spend two decades undercover documenting the lives of animals exploited for human gain. And nor would I wish to do it again.

The reality, though, is that our use – and abuse – of animals is vast and two decades is nowhere near enough time to fully examine the industries responsible for it. I've carried out investigations in more than thirty countries and yet only scratched the surface. There are billions of animals that I've never met but I know are being bred, reared or captured in the most tragic circumstances, sometimes hidden in plain sight, sometimes out of sight, and almost always out of mind.

But definitely hidden.

The people I've met, while all very different, have had one thing in common: a dislike of the public spotlight. They've wanted to stay in places away from people, away from newspapers, away from a national conversation. Most fly under the radar, safe in the knowledge that the only time the animals they're involved with will be shown to the public is when they're faceless on a supermarket shelf, draped off a coat hanger or manipulated as part of a short public performance. The public has just the narrowest of views into the lives of such animals, glimpsed only at times when they're least likely to ask questions. After all, people are hungry, or preoccupied with the acquisition of fashionable goods or they want to be entertained.

In my early days as a campaigner for animals, I thought I knew a lot about the way animals are treated. But I didn't. It wasn't until I began going undercover into the world of fur trapping and entering factory farms, slaughterhouses and circuses that I realised it was far worse than I could have imagined. And the more I discovered, the more I wanted to share so that people could make a more informed choice about their behaviour as consumers.

These stories are the result of citizen journalism. I never trained to report news, take pictures or record film. Instead, I taught myself to become a visual-evidence gatherer – a storyteller – who could find a way into the lives of others and unlock their secrets. And while I tried at first to do this openly, it quickly became clear to me that this approach wouldn't yield many results. The people I investigated wanted to remain hidden, so in turn I would have to hide amongst them.

Using cover stories to find information that otherwise isn't shared publicly was always an uncomfortable thing for me to do. But, without this approach, many important social justice issues would remain off limits to the public. It's always been clear to me that the plight of animals used by humans is a huge social justice issue that urgently needs addressing. I believe it's in the public interest to understand and know more about the lives of the sentient creatures we share this planet with and how our interaction with them can hurt us both. It's that belief that kept me digging for information, searching for ways to get inside places, and to meet the people responsible for these systems and practices.

By spending relatively long periods of time with some of my adversaries, I created a true picture of what life was like for the animals they incarcerated, trapped or killed. I also learned a lot about what they thought about their own role as the captor in this process. Perhaps unsurprisingly, most thought nothing of the animals that were the focus of their cruel behaviour. Some were indifferent to their charges, just ensuring they had food and water – enough to keep them alive – but that's where the relationship would end. There was little appreciation of their actual needs or that the barrenness of the animals' living conditions suppressed natural behaviours and affected their emotions. Then there were a few who genuinely seemed to like the animals on some level, despite what they subjected them to. One broiler chicken farmer in the USA that I met would, at the end of the day, bring a deck-chair and a beer into a shed crammed full of 30,000 chickens and enjoy just sitting there quietly watching them. He also dragged an oxygen respirator in with him. His chronic breathing difficulties were probably caused from the years he had spent working in those dusty, ammonia-heavy sheds. I wonder if he ever noticed the birds' own respiratory problems – a result of having been bred to grow super fast.

People can't always question why they do what they do. Sometimes it requires others to question before they can stop doing what they do or start thinking about things differently.

I certainly saw signs of that change during these projects, especially in the last few years. Factory farmers whose cage-rearing practices had been exposed are giving up; children expected to take on the family business are moving away, saying, 'Sorry folks, that's not for me.' And there is more happening at a legislative level: some countries, for instance, are introducing groundbreaking national legislation to end some of the worst treatment animals endure at the hands of humans.

Examples include banning fur farming, ending the testing of animals for cosmetics, and ending the culling of day-old male chicks for the egg industry.

Then there is the rise of veganism. For anyone who likes the taste of meat, current innovations in the manufacture of plant-based foods promise not only to look like meat but to taste like it too. Alternatively, real meat can now be grown in a lab, instead of on the body of a suffering animal. When price, taste and convenience converge for these cruelty-free foods in the not too distant future, then it's quite possible we'll see the end of factory farming. I strongly believe and hope that I'll see many dramatic changes for animals in my lifetime.

Knowing there is so much to be optimistic and hopeful about makes it a little easier for me to walk away from living a double life, masquerading as an investor, buyer or worker to get to the truth.

You see, witnessing cruelty to animals is very difficult to live with long term. I often revisit those moments when my instincts wanted me to intervene. Sometimes that was possible when I was alone, but most of the time it wasn't and when you've gone to such lengths to get yourself into a place where you can potentially show the world what happens to many animals when no one is looking, you need to fit in rather than draw attention to yourself. As a result, I have been able to help expose a lot of animal suffering, but I've also had to accept I usually couldn't intervene when I wanted to, so I've been left with a lot of chilling memories.

Investigating your adversaries is also exhausting. In some ways it's a bit like theatre. You're sitting in the front row of the audience and watching the cast perform. You're out of the spotlight, but only just; close enough to see everything, far enough not to be noticed. But when you're in the front row, you can easily get picked out. For me, those were the moments when my heart skipped a beat and I had to think on my feet to keep a story going, or face getting discovered.

There is also considerable risk and some danger that goes hand in hand with infiltrating people, industries and clandestine groups connected to animal suffering. Violence to animals is closely linked with violence to people, so I was particularly meticulous in my preparation for infiltration projects where, if I wasn't careful, I too could become a victim. Ensuring my cover story was watertight took some of the fear away, but a run of regular infiltration projects could be quite tough on the mind.

All these risks and concerns are multiplied the further away from home you are. The perils of working undercover in the UK seemed less significant because that is my home. I have a better understanding of working with, not against, the law here than I do in the USA, for example. The Ag-gag laws in some states of the USA, which forbid the act of undercover filming or photography on farms without the consent of their owner, could imprison someone like me. Such laws target potential whistle-blowers of animal rights abuses at these facilities; and, despite being described as a violation of the right to free speech and therefore a contravention of the First Amendment,[1] this legislation has not been overturned in every state. While the Ag-gag laws didn't stop me working there, when the law's not on your side from the outset, searching for the truth becomes more complicated, as well as playing havoc with your nerves.

In the autumn of 2018, I went to Kiev in Ukraine for my very last assignment. But, this time, it was to train fellow animal activists in the art of conducting undercover investigations. There are many new animal advocacy organisations, and

1. http://bit.ly/2PjdfeO

187

citizen journalists amongst them, keen to develop the use of undercover investigations to support their public outreach and political campaigning. This type of advocacy has played a key part in creating change for animals, particularly in the West, so it's heart-warming to see new organisations springing up all over the world, keen to put this pocket-powered technology to use, to do something good for animals.

But being an advocate for animals doesn't require you to go undercover on their behalf. You can start today by doing something small, like signing a petition or becoming a supporter of an animal protection organisation in your country working to end factory farming or the use of animals in fashion.

You might then want to get more active offline. You could show your support for animal issues by going along to a peaceful action or march, by becoming an organiser, or writing to political and corporate decision-makers. People power works, not always straightaway, but history shows us that strength and unity can bring something bad to an end, replacing it with something better.

And, remember, good people can do bad things but are usually capable of change if shown the right path in the right way. Tread lightly and always be compassionate to people, no matter what you know of them. Educate yourself, and plant the seeds of information respectfully. You, your activism and the animals will benefit from that approach.

If you're not vegan, give it a try. It's the most effective choice you can make as a consumer to limit animal suffering. There are some fantastic 'Try Vegan For A Month' pledges out there, like Veganuary, to get you started. They seek to both inspire and support people making this lifestyle change in a fun, kind and informative way. A cruelty-free lifestyle is very attainable these days and, with so many tasty plant-based food options available in many places around the world, it's not as challenging as it might once have been. Often, people start on the road to veganism when they realise that their choices as a consumer directly impact the lives of animals. They might decide to switch to free-range eggs, or wild-caught-only fish, or perhaps give up beef and lamb. From what I've seen, once we accept that animals' lives matter and we're honest with ourselves about the fact that we don't need flesh, eggs or dairy to survive – thrive even – it becomes impossible for us to justify continuing to consume those products. Whether they've made the change overnight, or taken little steps to cut cruelty out of their lives, many vegans share this sentiment: 'The only thing I regret about going vegan is that I didn't do it sooner.'

My activism for animals has moved into a new area. Instead of documenting animals in cages, I have turned to rescuing them from factory farms or neglectful owners. First a dog, then some cats, some chickens, some ducks and, most recently, another dog. There are seventeen right now and I fully expect there will be more arriving at our micro-sanctuary as time passes.

Actually, there's nothing I find more rewarding at the end of the day than sitting down in a deck-chair with a beer and watching the chickens and ducks just *being* chickens and ducks, not incarcerated in a factory farm, but free to roam without fear in their natural environment. If you have room for a rescue animal in your life, then you might just find adopting one will be the best thing you ever did.

We thrive with animals in our lives, but it must never be at their expense.

Acknowledgements

I'd like to thank all the undercover investigators I've worked with on assignments for animals over the years and also those that I don't know but who continue to do this work for all animals. In particular, I'd like to thank JT, SM, SG, LW, IS and GDS.

Special thanks to TV presenter and naturalist Chris Packham for his unwavering advocacy for all animals – big or small – and for kindly supporting this book by writing its foreword. And, to the campaigners with whom I've teamed up, who've supported my work or put great efforts into releasing it, to help secure change for animals: in particular, Leah Garcés and Joyce D'Silva.

For their interest and support in helping me share this project with others, many thanks to Jo-Anne McArthur and the team at We Animals, Ed Winters (Earthling Ed), Evanna Lynch (The Chickpeeps), Phillipa Smith (*Vegan Life* magazine), Maria Chiorando (Plant Based News), Matthew Glover and Jane Land (Veganuary), Isobel Davies and 'Bob' (who prefers to stay anonymous).

For correcting my abysmal grammar in the early drafts, many thanks to Hannah Yates, the first person outside of close family I felt able to share these previously closely guarded stories with.

For the beautiful works that adorn these pages, grateful thanks to the talented and compassionate illustrator Vita Sleigh.

For kindly backing my book, many thanks to every single patron named in this book, who was curious enough to want to know more about these stories and gave the book their support through the Unbound platform. Without them, this book would not exist.

Special thanks, also, to my parents and sister, who have always stood up for animals and who, in my early years, helped show me how to care for and defend them.

At Unbound, I'd like to thank particularly Sadie Mayne for her thoughtful advice and support during the structural edit, Josephine Salverda, Julia Koppitz and Sara Magness for helping me smoothly through the editorial process and Xander Cansell for commissioning.

And, last but not least, special thanks to my companion animals, whom I love dearly. They make me so happy but also act as a reminder of the suffering of others who have not had the fortune of being loved or treated with compassion.

Resources

The following organisations offer advice and support for people wanting to get more active on behalf of animals or in making the switch to cruelty-free living. Go check them out!

Non-profit organisations (NPOs)

Animal Aid: animalaid.org.uk
Animal Equality: animalequality.org
Animals Australia: animalsaustralia.org
Born Free Foundation: bornfree.org.uk
Compassion in World Farming: ciwf.org.uk
Cruelty Free International: crueltyfreeinternational.org
Djurens Ratt: djurensratt.se
Essere Animali: essereanimali.org
Freedom for Animals: freedomforanimals.org.uk
Gaia: gaia.be
L214: l214.com
Mercy for Animals: mercyforanimals.org
Obraz: obrancizvirat.cz
Otwarte Klatki: otwarteklatki.pl
Respect for Animals: respectforanimals.org

Surge Activism: surgeactivism.org
The Humane League: thehumaneleague.org
The Microsanctuary Movement: microsanctuary.org
The Vegan Society: vegansociety.com
Veganuary: veganuary.com
Veg Fund: vegfund.org
We Animals: weanimals.org
World Animal Protection: worldanimalprotection.org.uk

Podcasts

Earthling Ed/The Disclosure Podcast: https://open.spo-
tify.com/show/4O6snBhYYWQp90MVoBD-
Srq?si=f49jwh6YTA2UqmV1fZT4EQ
The Chickpeeps Podcast: https://www.thechickpeeps.com

Unbound is the world's first crowdfunding publisher.

We believe that wonderful things can happen when you clear a path for people who share a passion. That's why we've built a platform that brings together readers and authors to crowdfund books they believe in – and give fresh ideas that don't fit the traditional mould the chance they deserve.

This book is in your hands because readers made it possible. Everyone who pledged is listed at the front of the book and below. Join them by visiting unbound.com and supporting a book today.

Chrissianne Carpenter
Wendy Ann Carter
Samantha Chance
Slosh Chetty
Joey Cheung
Candace Chidiac
Katelyn Chisholm
Jenny Christie
Christine Chu
Jenna Church
Joanne Ciasulli
Gemma Clark
Clare Clemow
Sarah Cockerill
Lucianna Cole
Suzanne Coleman
David Coman-Hidy
Jack Common
Luissa Conlan
Harry Cooke
Thomas Cormack
Madelaine Couch
Josh Couchman
Gemma Cowin
Maxine Crinall
Valerie Daiber
Iva Damnjanovic
Tom Davies
Emma de Boer
Stephen Dent
Caroline Derry
Niki Dibble
Hannah Dickson
Vicki Doronina
Candice Dowson
May Duffy
Conor Duncan
Brandy Easter
Emma Eldridge
Stephen Elliott
Selene Ena
Ellie England
Annie Evans
Kellie Everson
Susan Fabrican
Virginia Fassnidge

Stephanie Faye
Emily Feins
Catherine Fendrich
Else Fergo
Lea Ferrante
Ashley & Drew Feuk
Anna Finch
Jennifer Fine
Sammantha Fisher
John Flack
Avery Florence
Genevieve Flowers
Friederike Foerster
Taylor Ford
Rebecca Fowles
Matthew Fox
Polly Fox
Pierre Frankignoul
Joshua Franklin
Jacqueline Franzen
Maurice Funnell
Lynn Gallagher
Kira Garcia
Miranda Garner
Michael Genner
Phoebe Gerrard
Laura Gibbons
Isadora Godoy
Melissa Gohlke
Daniela Gottschalk
Luna Grant
Elin Green
Aurélia Greff
Julie Hargreaves
Candice Haridimou
Max Harris
Chelsea Harrop
Lee Hawkins
Fiaah Heffernan
Christopher Hendrickson
Tom Hendry
Charlotte Hewitt
Theresa Higginson
Michael Hileski
Samantha Hockley
Emma Hoel

Emma Hollingshead
Mags Hopwood
Ewelina Hornicka
Susie Humphrys
Jordan Hunt
Nanie Hurley
Ae Iou
Laura-Jayne Ireton
Zoe Jackson
L. Jackson-Cristal
Chuck Jesse
Leanna Jones
Craig Jones and Rosie Jones
Sarah Kanti
Jenna Keating
Felicitas Keil
Ella Kennedy
Cyrus Kiani
Gavin Kisley
Schmidt Klara
Mahi Klosterhalfen
Sarrah Koheeallee
Claudia Kolts
Tracy Lai
Macey Laidlaw
Rich Larsen
Geert Laugs
Dylan Lemonsky
Janosch Linkersdörfer
Andrea Lloyd
Fiona Longin
Michelle Loulis
Rebecca Lowans
Emma Lowe
Angel Lugo
Jenica Lyon Clapsaddle
Mairead Lyons
Annalise Mancinelli
Jacob Mandry
Kate Marie O'donoghue
Melissa Marlow
R.P.K Marshall
George Marshall
Siobhan Martin
Kyle Martyn-Clark
Helen Marvell

Becky Matthews
Jo-Anne McArthur
Michele McDonald
Carole McIntosh
Jo McLean
Karen McNicol
Laurie Michaels
Petr Michalec
Jeni Miles
Barbora Misakova
Phillipa Mitchell
Sonja Mitrovic
Megan Moore
Ann Moorhouse
Veronica Morales
Amanda Moreland
Melissa Morrissey
Lana Moss
Alison Myles
Hanna Nassar
Carlo Navato
Sasha Tracy Newton
Birgit Nurmela
Kerri O'Brien
John Oberg
Damaris Ollervides
Ana Ortega
Eric Ossenfort
Katelyn Owens
Ann Oyediran
Robert Page
Anna Palmer
Jared Pardi
Kunjal Patel
Lauren Pearce
Chris Pearson
Annika Pellegrini
Anja Peterson
Joana Pimenta Lemos
Caroline Piper
Sarah Plumer
Kat Podgorski
Kelsey Poli
Danie Poolman
Hilary Potts
Lisa Powers

Hima Prasad
Janet Price
Melissa Ramplin
Ralph Reed
Gary Reynolds
Lex Rigby
Louise Riley
Jo Robbins
Lisa Roebuck-Krasno
Judit Ruiz Ricart
Amber Rusk Davies
Niki Rust
Emma Ruth
Cheryl Rutherford
Kieran Ryan
Hoshimi Sakai
Melissa Salmon
Rosa Sari
Melanie Savage
Jan Schaffer
Lucy Schoeman
Serena Serena
Harish Sethu
Evan Shamoon
Jen Sheil
Laura Shields
Derek Shiller
Albana Shosholli Fridström
Rae Sibbitt
Charlotte Skerratt
Nina Skyttmo
Sid Smallman
Martin Smedjeback
Alacoque Smedley
Wendy Smith
Carrie Smith
Sofia Pipera Sofia Pipera
Rebecca Sommerville
Lost Souljah
Jen Spears
Calum Spence
Lyn Stephens
Kristen Sterner
Christine Stockman
Gilly Stoddart

Trevor Stoddart
Joachim Stoeber
Anna Strong
Ronja Svensson
Zanna Swijngedouw
Dimosthenis Syriopoulos
Amelie Taillon
Hayley Tait
Lynn Telford
Aimee Theresa
Claire Thomas
Leah Traub
Alvaro Trujillo Olaiz
Tia Turner
Tia Turner
Rebecca van Eijden
Mariska van Geelen
Ad Veg-fruitarian
Louise Virgo
Ilaria Vista
Rosanna Vista
Kaitlyn Warick
Kristin Wasiluk
Craig Waters
Susannah Waters
Aimee Weir
Zoe West
Lottie Williams
Becca Williams
David Willis
Lauren Wills
Bogna Wiltowska
Michael Winter
Val Wolf
Yenna Wolf
Florence Wolff
Teri Worthington
Jules Wright
Julia Wright
Gabriela Wurzinger
Nicole Yam
Stuart Yates
Andrew Young
Iryna Yzon
Bartek Zając